SUTLIFFIAN DEEP DIVE DEVOTIONALS

EXODUS:
A JOURNEY OF FAITH

Book 2

Paul Sutliff

Copyright © 2024 Sutliffian Press

All rights reserved.

No part of this book may be reproduced, stored in a retrieval system, or transmitted by any means, electronic, mechanical, photocopying, recording, or otherwise, without written permission from the author.

ISBN (Paperback): 979-8-9921204-5-5
ISBN (eBook): 979-8-9921204-4-8

To the Reader:

It is my sincere wish that this book will help you grow in your faith. Each daily devotion you will find inside was a part of my own daily devotions. I believe that it takes dedication and motivation to serve the one and only King of all creation, the Lord Jesus Christ. In reading this devotional, set aside the same time each day. Include a wake-up prayer before devotions, giving praise to Jesus for another day to give him the glory.

Forward

This book is dedicated to those who are disciples in Christ. It was written for YOU! You are about to embark on a journey of depth in scripture reading. Each day's devotional was part of my personal study. I spent the time to not only read the scripture, but to look at commentaries, to study words and their meanings. I looked at context. Asked questions. Why? Because I believe the Word of God is so important, we have to dig into it to get as much as we can out of it.

What appears a short reading actually takes me about an hour. Prayer, reading His Word, studying the passages, making sure I don't go to fast, have done one important thing to my life. I hold each reading in my heart most of the day. Better yet, each reading serves to arm me for battle, by making scripture not only real, but places the Word in my heart so that I may give answers to those who have questions.

For those struggling with anything some call addictions, which I call binding sin, I believe a daily deep-dive into HIS Word, is the solution. You want out of the sin that binds you to return to it? Grab one of these devotionals. Dig into the Word of God, pray and meditate on what you read. I promise your life will be better. I can say this because my life blossomed as if I had no clue to the wonders of God, before I started this part of my life.

For those scared of doing anything in depth – I am a Special Education Teacher. I write to average people, not scholars. This book was meant for you. It is purposefully written simply for the intent of sharing the deepness and joy of reading God's Word.

If you are a pastor or chaplain doing a prison ministry and are looking for a discount on books. Please contact me at Berean_research@yahoo.com.

DAY #51
EXODUS 17:1-7

1 And all the congregation of the children of Israel journeyed from the wilderness of Sin, after their journeys, according to the commandment of the LORD, and pitched in Rephidim: and *there was* no water for the people to drink.
2 Wherefore the people did chide with Moses, and said, Give us water that we may drink. And Moses said unto them, Why chide you with me? wherefore do you tempt the LORD?
3 And the people thirsted there for water; and the people murmured against Moses, and said, Wherefore *is* this *that* you hast brought us up out of Egypt, to kill us and our children and our cattle with thirst?
4 And Moses cried unto the LORD, saying, What shall I do unto this people? they be almost ready to stone me.
5 And the LORD said unto Moses, Go on before the people, and take with you of the elders of Israel; and your rod, wherewith you smote the river, take in your hand, and go.
6 Behold, I will stand before you there upon the rock in Horeb; and you shalt smite the rock, and there shall come water out of it, that the people may drink. And Moses did so in the sight of the elders of Israel.
7 And he called the name of the place Massah, and Meribah, because of the chiding of the children of Israel, and because they tempted the LORD, saying, Is the LORD among us, or not?

It is interesting that the people of Israel, the Hebrew people, are complaining to Moses and not going before God on their own and praying to Him. While they were oppressed, they individually called out to God in their need. What was stopping them? Had they forgotten that the God they cried out to in need was a personal God who delivered them?

Moses is given very specific directions when he goes before the Lord. He follows through and smites the rock. Water comes forth. But the miracle to Moses is not that water came forth. No, it is that God did not discipline rebellious people who questioned whether he was present with them when he fed them daily and led them as a pillar of cloud during the day. They still seem unaware of who God is. They seem unaware that they, too, can seek out God. The polytheist gods, the gods of the Egyptians, were impersonal. They needed a priest or a person to stand between them and the men. Those gods were fickle and not above acting foolish with emotions and committing what men would call sins. So they seem to think that God would lead them someplace to die and abandon them. This unknowable, impersonable God that delivered them out of slavery was not what they thought. He attempted to get them to call on Him, not Moses. What would have happened if the people had come to Moses and asked him to lead them in praying to God for water? Instead of complaining?

Do you complain when you can simply go to God in prayer? Think about this as a missed opportunity given to the children of Israel. It was a chance for them to unite in prayer. Are you facing something that should cause you to pray instead of complain?

Dear Lord Jesus,

Help me to leave complaining aside and instead begin to seek You. Help me to see these times as chances to seek You out for answers and miracles of providence. Help me to see the relationship you are trying to establish in my life. Help my prayer life to grow. Cause me to seek you out in prayer more and more. Lord, you know I am not begging for hardship. I am asking for reminders to seek you out. Reminders not to complain but to seek your face. Lord, let me become that example of seeking you out and putting away complaining.

In Jesus name, Amen.

DAY #52
EXODUS 17:8-16

8   Then came Amalek, and fought with Israel in Rephidim.
9   And Moses said unto Joshua, Choose us out men, and go out, fight with Amalek: to morrow I will stand on the top of the hill with the rod of God in mine hand.
10 So Joshua did as Moses had said to him, and fought with Amalek: and Moses, Aaron, and Hur went up to the top of the hill.
11 And it came to pass, when Moses held up his hand, that Israel prevailed: and when he let down his hand, Amalek prevailed.
12 But Moses' hands *were* heavy; and they took a stone, and put *it* under him, and he sat thereon; and Aaron and Hur stayed up his hands, the one on the one side, and the other

	on the other side; and his hands were steady until the going down of the sun.
13	And Joshua discomfited Amalek and his people with the edge of the sword.
14	And the LORD said unto Moses, Write this *for* a memorial in a book, and rehearse *it* in the ears of Joshua: for I will utterly put out the remembrance of Amalek from under heaven.
15	And Moses built an altar, and called the name of it Jehovahnissi:
16	For he said, Because the LORD hath sworn *that* the LORD *will have* war with Amalek from generation to generation.

Interestingly, the first people to react to the presence of a large group of "refugees" did not approach them and ask how they might help, as many would nowadays. They observed the people who came out of the sea and saw many odd things, making them wonder if they were a threat. These people appeared most strangely; they came out of the sea! They were strangers, yet, they did not have to forage for food to feed their people. Oh, they sent out scouts that ate a little here and there, but this huge group of people were reported as surviving in areas with no food! If this was true, perhaps they brought large stores of food.

Would the presence of a group about 2 million in size be a threat to a local civilization? Yes, based on food availability. They could be seen as a potential drain on the available resources. Worse, it is likely that they would be ravenously hungry by the time they left the Wilderness! Wouldn't it be better to attack them while they were hungry? It would be a quick and easy annihilation, then, right?

But things were not as they seemed. The people who came out of the sea survived because their God loved them. This battle was not with weary, hungry people at all. They were healthy and strong but had no battle skills.

The idea that the conflict was still raging based on what Moses was doing was not lost on the Hebrews. Afterward, when reflecting on this, Moses sets up an altar, a place to give offerings unto the Lord—naming the place "Jehovah-Nissi," meaning The Lord our Banner. The Israelites did not have a flag, a pennant, or anything to war under. Possibly, the other side had many banners proclaiming their gods. The Hebrew people came and fought without a single banner. Why? Because the LORD God who delivered them out of the hand of the Egyptians was their banner!

Dear Lord Jesus,

Help me, Lord, in my unbelief to remember you alone have saved me and that I have done nothing to deserve your great love. That makes You the God who fights for me. You are my banner. Never let me forget that you, oh Lord, are the one to whom I owe everything.

In Jesus', Amen.

DAY #53
EXODUS 18:1-12

1   When Jethro, the priest of Midian, Moses' father in law, heard of all that God had done for Moses, and for Israel his people, *and* that the LORD had brought Israel out of Egypt;
2   Then Jethro, Moses' father in law, took Zipporah, Moses' wife, after he had sent her back,
3   And her two sons; of which the name of the one *was* Gershom; for he said, I have been an alien in a strange land:
4   And the name of the other *was* Eliezer; for the God of my father, *said he, was* mine help, and delivered me from the sword of Pharaoh:
5   And Jethro, Moses' father in law, came with his sons and his wife unto Moses into the wilderness, where he encamped at the mount of God:
6   And he said unto Moses, I your father in law Jethro am come unto you, and your wife, and her two sons with her.
7   And Moses went out to meet his father in law, and did obeisance, and kissed him; and they asked each other of *their* welfare; and they came into the tent.
8   And Moses told his father in law all that the LORD had done unto Pharaoh and to the Egyptians for Israel's sake, *and* all the travail that had come upon them by the way, and *how* the LORD delivered them.
9   And Jethro rejoiced for all the goodness which the LORD had done to Israel, whom he had delivered out of the hand of the Egyptians.
10 And Jethro said, Blessed *be* the LORD, who hath delivered you out of the hand of the Egyptians, and out of the hand of Pharaoh, who hath delivered the people from under the hand of the Egyptians.

11 Now I know that the LORD *is* greater than all gods: for in the thing wherein they dealt proudly *he was* above them.

12 And Jethro, Moses' father in law, took a burnt offering and sacrifices for God: and Aaron came, and all the elders of Israel, to eat bread with Moses' father in law before God.

DAY #54
EXODUS 18:13-27

13 And it came to pass on the morrow, that Moses sat to judge the people: and the people stood by Moses from the morning unto the evening.

14 And when Moses' father in law saw all that he did to the people, he said, What *is* this thing that you do to the people? why do you sit yourself alone, and all the people stand by you from morning unto even?

15 And Moses said unto his father in law, Because the people come unto me to enquire of God:

16 When they have a matter, they come unto me; and I judge between one and another, and I do make *them* know the statutes of God, and his laws.

17 And Moses' father in law said unto him, The thing that you do *is* not good.

18 You will surely wear away, both you, and this people that *is* with you: for this thing *is* too heavy for you; you are not able to perform it yourself alone.

19 Hearken now unto my voice, I will give you counsel, and God shall be with you: Be you for the people to God-ward, that you mayest bring the causes unto God:

20	And you shalt teach them ordinances and laws, and shalt show them the way wherein they must walk, and the work that they must do.
21	Moreover you shall provide out of all the people able men, such as fear God, men of truth, hating covetousness; and place *such* over them, *to be* rulers of thousands, *and* rulers of hundreds, rulers of fifties, and rulers of tens:
22	And let them judge the people at all seasons: and it shall be, *that* every great matter they shall bring unto you, but every small matter they shall judge: so shall it be easier for yourself, and they shall bear *the burden* with you.
23	If you shall do this thing, and God command you *so*, then you shalt be able to endure, and all this people shall also go to their place in peace.
24	So Moses hearkened to the voice of his father in law, and did all that he had said.
25	And Moses chose able men out of all Israel, and made them heads over the people, rulers of thousands, rulers of hundreds, rulers of fifties, and rulers of tens.
26	And they judged the people at all seasons: the hard causes they brought unto Moses, but every small matter they judged themselves.
27	And Moses let his father in law depart; and he went his way into his own land.

Can you imagine this? One man over 2 million people. Only one man is acting as a judge! When you think that big about this, the entire concept is indeed wearisome. Jethro's wisdom is very important here. In the beginning, Moses was afraid to do things alone. He had his brother Aaron help him. But in matters of judgment, he suddenly was alone again. Maybe Moses had grown confident in his ability to serve God in this role. Looking from the outside, sometimes things are easier to see and understand in terms of fixing things. Jethro's wisdom here impacts all of Israel, not just Moses when you think about this. If each leader also served God like Moses and spent time teaching and training others about how to live – wouldn't that make life as a whole for the entire people of Israel better?

As you read this, you have to think, wait, God has not given the Ten Commandments yet! So can you imagine the continued frustration when judging those who broke basic social rules? Now with the additional helpers who would not only judge but help others to learn how to live and were chosen based on their own lives being examples, life in general for all had to improve. This could have been a huge sigh of relief when expectations were revealed down to the lowest levels.

In businesses, when high expectations are shared at all levels, your quality goes up! The same happens when teachers have high expectations of students. People rise to higher expectations. Good teachers help those having difficulty. Good students help their friends raise themselves to achieve those higher expectations.

Ultimately, the Israelites must have had such a deep and great love for Moses' father-in-law Jethro. For this tidbit of wisdom echoed throughout all of Israel when it was implemented. Jethro, the priest of Midian, knew God. He knew this great and loving God and would not be silent when he saw something that needed to be done better. Can you imagine the impact of Christians living like this today?

Dear Lord Jesus,

Please help me grow in wisdom and understanding of Your Word. May that be first and foremost in my life? May my knowledge of Your Word first influence my own life and then be shared with my family and then with the others in my life. May Your Word become that which not only changes my life for the better but also changes those around me. May my continual joy in Your Word become so abundant in my nature, and the need to share Your wonders teem up within me, not allowing me to be silent. So your joy may be heard in abundance.

In Jesus name, Amen.

DAY #55
EXODUS 19:1-8

1   In the third month, when the children of Israel were gone forth out of the land of Egypt, the same day came they *into* the wilderness of Sinai.
2   For they were departed from Rephidim, and were come *to* the desert of Sinai, and had pitched in the wilderness; and there Israel camped before the mount.
3   And Moses went up unto God, and the LORD called unto him out of the mountain, saying, Thus shalt you say to the house of Jacob, and tell the children of Israel;
4   You have seen what I did unto the Egyptians, and *how* I bare you on eagles' wings, and brought you unto myself.

5	Now therefore, if you will obey my voice indeed, and keep my covenant, then you shall be a peculiar treasure unto me above all people: for all the earth *is* mine:
6	And you shall be unto me a kingdom of priests, and an holy nation. These *are* the words which you shalt speak unto the children of Israel.
7	And Moses came and called for the elders of the people, and laid before their faces all these words which the LORD commanded him.
8	And all the people answered together, and said, All that the LORD hath spoken we will do. And Moses returned the words of the people unto the LORD.

This is a call and response from God to the people of Israel. God says to the children of Israel:

If you will obey my voice indeed, and keep my covenant, then you shall be a peculiar treasure unto me above all people: for all the earth is mine.

The people respond, "All that the LORD has spoken we will do."

Maybe most people will miss this one. Maybe not, but the words God asks have to do with the future. It is directed towards following HIM in the future. The people respond by saying, "we will do all you have said" (past tense). Maybe they were stating there is nothing hard that has been asked of them yet. So yes, they will gladly follow him. Remember all that they had been told as far as how to behave, and more had been passed down to them through generations. Moses had been working on teaching them these things. This response stops short of stating, "Yes, Lord, we will listen to YOUR voice and obey YOUR covenant." It can also be said that sometimes we say things that do not necessarily communicate everything we intend to communicate. God knows our hearts. He knows what we truly mean. When we say yes, and our heart is saying, "no way," He knows. It is that plain and simple.

The people had been delivered from centuries of slavery, watched God work his wonders, and saw HIM act as their mighty and strong tower in time of need. They saw HIM provide food to meet their needs each day. This response lacks energy and seems hesitant for a people whom God has protected and continues to protect.

Think how you would respond if God asked you this question today.

Dear Lord Jesus,

You know my heart. You know where I stand more than I do myself. Lord, mold me and make me be one who seeks after the desires of YOUR heart rather than my own. Help me to say, "YES, LORD, I WILL FOLLOW YOU AND OBEY THAT WHICH YOU ASK OF ME!

In Jesus name, Amen.

DAY #56
EXODUS 19:9-19

9   And the LORD said unto Moses, Lo, I come unto you in a thick cloud, that the people may hear when I speak with you, and believe you forever. And Moses told the words of the people unto the LORD.

10   And the LORD said unto Moses, Go unto the people, and sanctify them to day and tomorrow, and let them wash their clothes,

11   And be ready against the third day: for the third day the LORD will come down in the sight of all the people upon mount Sinai.

12   And you shalt set bounds unto the people round about, saying, Take heed to yourselves, *that you* go *not* up into the mount, or touch the border of it: whosoever touches the mount shall be surely put to death:

13   There shall not an hand touch it, but he shall surely be stoned, or shot through; whether *it be* beast or man, it shall not live: when the trumpet sounds long, they shall come up to the mount.

14   And Moses went down from the mount unto the people, and sanctified the people; and they washed their clothes.

15   And he said unto the people, Be ready against the third day: come not at *your* wives.

16   And it came to pass on the third day in the morning, that there were thunders and lightnings, and a thick cloud upon the mount, and the voice of the trumpet exceeding loud; so that all the people that *was* in the camp trembled.

17   And Moses brought forth the people out of the camp to meet with God; and they stood at the nether part of the mount.

18   And mount Sinai was altogether on a smoke, because the LORD descended upon it in fire: and the smoke thereof ascended as the smoke of a furnace, and the whole mount quaked greatly.
19   And when the voice of the trumpet sounded long, and waxed louder and louder, Moses spake, and God answered him by a voice.

Can you imagine being told to prepare to meet the living God? Would you do so in fear and love? You know that this God has done great things for you and your people. You know that he provided your food daily. Wouldn't you want to meet Him? As the short time in preparation became shorter and shorter, what would you be thinking of? Would you be shaking? Would you be fearful of the numerous things you've done in the past that you know were not only wrong but horrifyingly wrong? Would you be begging for forgiveness so you could be in God's presence – a place you think must be peaceful and terrible to those not prepared to meet him?

As part of the preparation, they had to clean their clothes. In most situations, this task would fall to the wife. Yet, in this case, the task is of such great importance you wonder if there are many more men taking part in this task, not only because there are men who are single, but because of the need to be ready to do what God has asked.

You wait for the third day. That day the mountain explodes in thunder and lightning. Yet, those acts of violence stay there. It's like a display that says, "Yes, I AM HERE!"

Then the sound of a trumpet, a sound so loud and powerful it goes through you. You can no longer deny that you are afraid. You feel this sense of minuteness about yourself. You are a puny spec compared to the vastness of your God.

Next, Moses calls you out. Come to see the mountain. Come to be present in the presence of God. Something you wish for and fear all at the same time.

What would have been your reaction after seeing the pillar of fire that had led you by night? To some, that pillar, indeed would have been scary and fearful. Would you have wondered if your work cleaning YOUR clothes was good enough? Would the weight of your sins have you bent over in the presence of THE holy God?

You watch as Moses talks to God, then this fire – this living presence of God answers him! It must have been something to see someone having a conversation with God, especially being able to hear both sides.

Dear Lord Jesus,

You are the all-powerful, all-mighty God. My heart longs to be in your presence, yet I know that doing as you desire and being the man/woman you want me to be is the best way others can see You. Help me, Lord, that I may leave those things behind that do not allow YOU to shine through me. I ask Lord that change me. Mold me into a better person. Take away my vanity and self-seeking desires that YOU alone are glorified. Purify my words. Remove my impure thoughts that my only expression may be of Your love.

In Jesus name, Amen.

DAY #57
EXODUS 19:20-25

20 And the LORD came down upon mount Sinai, on the top of the mount: and the LORD called Moses *up* to the top of the mount; and Moses went up.
21 And the LORD said unto Moses, Go down, charge the people, lest they break through unto the LORD to gaze, and many of them perish.
22 And let the priests also, which come near to the LORD, sanctify themselves, lest the LORD break forth upon them.
23 And Moses said unto the LORD, The people cannot come up to mount Sinai: for you charged us, saying, Set bounds about the mount, and sanctify it.
24 And the LORD said unto him, Away, get you down, and you shalt come up, you, and Aaron with you: but let not the priests and the people break through to come up unto the LORD, lest he break forth upon them.
25 So Moses went down unto the people, and spake unto them.

While Moses was told to do this for the sake of the people, he knew that if they disobeyed – someone would die. Somehow this had to be in the back of his head buzzing about. Moses had the job of being God's frontman. He was their priest. This means he was attuned to the needs of the people. He listened to them and constantly scanned them as he watched. He was ready to help.

God needed Moses' full attention this time. Moses had completed all of God's requests and created some warnings for people not to stray beyond. Yet, somehow this also must have been a distraction to Moses. The closest thing I can equate it to is the role of the head usher during the church service. Head ushers are supposed to be aware of everything in the church. They are supposed to see it all, all at once. If you are in this role, you do this activity out of love for the Lord God as part of your service to Him. Moses had been leading the Israelites for some time, all day, every day. It may have even been so ingrained in him that he did this unconsciously.

In simple terms, Moses needed a "Reset" or "ReStart." Moses goes down and speaks to the people. He says what God has told them and returns to the presence of God with his brother Aaron. Sometimes, all we need to set things right is to walk away and restart what we left. That brief walk away and back seems to get us right where we need to be. Gamers, writers, and so many more grasp this concept.

Dear Lord Jesus!

You know us so well; you know where our hearts are at. You know if we are distracted. You know what it takes to put us back on track. Lord, there are many in our lives we love and pray for. Some have said they love you and have gone off track. Lord, give them a reset and put them back on the path to loving you. Lord, reset me also. Make me think more of You than ever before. Help me to see how You are worthy of my full attention.

In Jesus name, Amen.

DAY #58
EXODUS 20:1-7

1. And God spake all these words, saying,
2. I *am* the LORD your God, which have brought you out of the land of Egypt, out of the house of bondage.
3. You shalt have no other gods before me.
4. You shalt not make unto you any graven image, or any likeness *of any thing* that *is* in heaven above, or that *is* in the earth beneath, or that *is* in the water under the earth:
5. You shalt not bow down yourself to them, nor serve them: for I the LORD your God *am* a jealous God, visiting the iniquity of the fathers upon the children unto the third and fourth *generation* of them that hate me;
6. And shewing mercy unto thousands of them that love me, and keep my commandments.
7. You shalt not take the name of the LORD your God in vain; for the LORD will not hold him guiltless that takes his name in vain.

This begins the 10 commandments. Here are the first three.

1. You shall have no other gods before me.
2. You shall not make idols nor bow down to them.
3. You shall not take the name of the Lord your God in vain.

I remember being surprised to learn that Catholics had a different set of the Ten Commandments. In my mind, I asked how that was possible. We had the same Bible, right? I had so much to learn. How could these things GOD considered most important be twisted and lied about so easily? Better still, the question that truly bothered me was, why would anyone accept this? It comes down to reading God's Word. We are fifty-seven days into reading the book of Exodus and praying about HIS WORD! That is what this comes down to. Why do people accept lies? Because they do not know the truth for themselves or fear being harmed for telling what is true.

I remember teaching my children about idols and how they are against God's commandments. Some we called Isis. As the kids grew older, they asked questions about how it was possible for a "church" to have idols when they claimed they teach the Bible? I told them the difference is simple. It is all about who reads the Bible.

These first three commandments are all about us recognizing who God is. He should be first and foremost in our lives. We should see him as holy and pure. We should see him as having greatness and love beyond our description. Could we put anything before a God like this? Could we take HIS name in vain?

Some grew up in homes where the Lord's name was taken in vain so often that you thought it was a normal part of conversation. But as you learned it was wrong, you started to change how you talk. It might have even seemed painful to continually hear others talking like this. Why? Because it is one of the first commands given to us to obey to NOT use his name in vain.

Three commandments direct us to remember who God is and to treat him as above ourselves. That's all just three. There is no demand on how you must say as you pray or what you must do as you pray. When you think about these three commandments, you learn that they are given by a loving God. A God who desires to be first in your life. A God who deserves to be first in your life because there are no other gods! There is no one more worthy than HIM.

Dear Lord Jesus!

You alone are worthy of my praise. There is none like You! You deserve my attention. You deserve my devotion. No one is as patient with me as you are. When I do things I know are wrong, You wait for me to come to you and beg for forgiveness. But this does not keep you from making things happen for me that protect me and keep me safe. Your loving arms and your strong embrace are always there for me. Help me to share that with others. Help me to share this love of yours because it is so much bigger than me.

In Jesus name, Amen.

DAY #59
EXODUS 20:8-11

8 Remember the sabbath day, to keep it holy.
9 Six days shalt you labour, and do all your work:
10 But the seventh day *is* the sabbath of the LORD your God: *in it* you shalt not do any work, you, nor your son, nor your daughter, your manservant, nor your maidservant, nor your cattle, nor your stranger that *is* within your gates:
11 For *in* six days the LORD made heaven and earth, the sea, and all that in them *is*, and rested the seventh day: wherefore the LORD blessed the sabbath day, and hallowed it.

There are some things that make you wonder. The Sabbath Day, the importance of rest and taking a breather, is ingrained throughout Judaism. It's the fourth commandment! Its importance is shown by God resting on the Seventh Day. In Christian circles, the day of rest moves to the first day because that is the day Jesus rose from the dead. On that day, we also gather to worship. Yet there are some to whom Sundays are not a day of rest – your pastors. They in turn take off another day in the week.

One of the things that has been learned in brain research is there is great value in rest. Your ability to learn new things depends on utilizing rest. What does this say about those who are "workaholics"? Will they suffer something mentally for not taking a break? The answer is that mental breakdowns can happen because of it.

The seventh day is a reminder of who our Creator is. – on Sundays, we still celebrate the Creator, but we celebrate HIM in name, as the second person of the Godhead, Jesus! Are you taking time to rest and celebrate God's love for you? Did you rest this Sunday?

Dear Lord Jesus,

Lord, thank you for giving importance to rest. You truly know us better than we know ourselves. Many of us have difficulty resting. We feel guilty about it. But then, if even YOU rested, we should acknowledge the importance of rest. Science is slowly catching up to your wisdom. Now it places importance on rest. Lord, help us to direct our thoughts to you on that special day. Let our worship and praise glorify You on the day of rest and not ourselves.

In Jesus name, Amen.

DAY #60
EXODUS 20:12

12   Honour your father and your mother: that your days may be long upon the land which the LORD your God gives you.

This is the only commandment that comes with a reward for its obedience. It is also unique in that this commandment, which instructs us to obey our parents, instructs us to honor them rather than obey them. Honoring your parents has to do with a lot more than obeying them. As a child, this can not be known. But when you get older, you become parents and then find yourselves saying the same things your parents said to you. Sometimes that makes you mad, and sometimes that makes you laugh. As life goes on and age sets in for you and your parents, you enter a role where you need to help your parents because they actually need your help. An honor like this is then a life experience, it is not an either/or in the immediate present. Rather it is a series of events that includes your choice to listen to your parents and obey. It includes you finding your parents' sayings in your mouth as you raise your own children. Then it is in how you treat your elderly parents who need your help. If this passage had simply said to obey your parents, it would have been meant for children only. But no, this is meant for everyone, both children and adults. Even when parents are gone, how you honor that memory plays a part.

The reward promised here reflects your ability to honor your parents. For children to honor, it means obedience. For young adults to honor, it often means listening to and following their advice. As life goes on, it means staying in touch and sharing your joys with your parents. As life goes on and you realize your mother or father needs help in something, you simply do it. Sometimes this means helping them take care of things they used to do themselves quite well. Sometimes it means finding help for them to continue living a good life. That can mean a lot of different things. Then, of course, when your parents have left this earth, how do you tell others about them? How do you honor them then?

Ask yourself today, how am I honoring my parents?

Dear Lord Jesus,

Help me to honor my parents. Help me to do that which is right by them. I may not be the best child, but I want to honor my parents. Lord, show me how to do this best, whether it is by obeying, listening, or any other way. Work on me and make me a better example of your love by doing this better.

In Jesus name, Amen.

DAY #61
EXODUS 20:13-16

13   You shalt not kill.
14   You shalt not commit adultery.
15   You shalt not steal.
16   You shalt not bear false witness against your neighbor.

These four commandments need no explanation. They address things we immediately recognize as sinful, wrong, and evil. There are some out there who like to claim that all morals and all sense of what is right and wrong are all related to culture and situation. This is often done to put God in a box. Yes, it means to make Him smaller than HE is. Yet, there are moral laws that are present in everyone from birth 'til death. These 4 commandments need no explanation since they are part of those moral laws that reside within us.

Another way to see the Ten Commandments is that they are given in order of importance. They start with giving God the glory and honor he is due. Four commandments do this. The fifth commandment places importance on the role parents play. These commandments should be easy to follow if the first five are followed by the parents showing their children how they should live. It would then be unthinkable that these four commandments should be thought of as something okay.

Some argue that anyone who violates these commandments, on which every country has laws, has low self-esteem. The claim is that criminals do not place a high value on themselves. The truth is, however, the opposite of this. People who violate these commandments intentionally think more highly of themselves than of others. There are actual scientific articles written that prove this. This leads us back to how the first four commandments have to be ignored in order to get here. Then looking at the fifth commandment with respect to honoring your parents.

Children have to be taught what property is. They have to be taught what cultures believe about property. There are no cultures without rules on this. There are some cultures that teach theft as a way of life. But this brings us back up top, asking if they value themselves above others. Why is this important? Because the God of the Christians valued not Himself above others. He gave HIS life so that we may live life eternally. How can we not live as He asks?

Dear Lord Jesus,

Help me to live for You! Help me to keep You first and foremost in my life. Help me to honor my parents so that You also may be praised. Lord, guide my choices so that Your will remains first and foremost in how I live. Lord, let this life You desire for me be a living example to those who do not know You.

In Jesus name, Amen.

DAY #62
EXODUS 20:17

17   You shalt not covet thy neighbour's house, thou shalt not covet thy neighbour's wife, nor his manservant, nor his maidservant, nor his ox, nor his ass, nor any thing that *is* your neighbour's.

This commandment, which appears to be the smallest of them all, is, in some ways, the most instructive. This is the only commandment where your thoughts are revealed as possibly sinful. Until now, no one condemns a man's or a woman's thoughts. Perhaps we should have had a clue since God says in the first commandment that he wants to be first in your life. How else could he know if he was not talking about your thoughts? Coveting is not being lustful. Lust is the next step – it signifies an overwhelming desire. This is simply the beginning of what creates lust. Up to this moment, the Israelites likely thought obeying God was simple. Now they see Him as the one who knows their thoughts too. Let's face it, some of our thoughts are not close to pure.

Most of our sins are the result of our thoughts. We think too about doing something we know is wrong. We may think of it at a glance at first, then we revisit that thought. Then over and over, play that thought. Suddenly we act on that thought. When we do this, we frequently remind ourselves that we are doing something wrong. Then having done so, we hang our heads in shame.

God is giving us a tool here to stop us from sinning. Don't think about the things we know we should not do. Don't desire those sins, for even that desire is a sin. If we think of our thoughts as having the power to sin and having the power to stop sin, we now have a new toolset to help us stay on track with the things God desires for us.

Dear Lord Jesus,

Be Lord of my thoughts. Be the one who has charge over all of my mind. Remove those thoughts I should not have. Lord, I do not want thoughts that separate me from Your love. Sin does that. I get it. So I ask again Lord, for You to be Lord of my thoughts. Help set a guard in my mind that I should not think about things that are not pleasing to you.

In Jesus' name, Amen.

DAY #63
EXODUS 20:18-26

18   And all the people saw the thunderings, and the lightnings, and the noise of the trumpet, and the mountain smoking: and when the people saw *it*, they removed, and stood afar off.

19   And they said unto Moses, Speak you with us, and we will hear: but let not God speak with us, lest we die.

20   And Moses said unto the people, Fear not: for God is come to prove you, and that his fear may be before your faces, that you sin not.

21   And the people stood afar off, and Moses drew near unto the thick darkness where God *was*.

22   And the LORD said unto Moses, Thus you shalt say unto the children of Israel, You have seen that I have talked with you from heaven.

23   You shall not make with me gods of silver, neither shall you make unto you gods of gold.

24   An altar of earth you shalt make unto me, and shalt sacrifice thereon your burnt offerings, and your peace offerings, your sheep, and your oxen: in all places where I record my name I will come unto you, and I will bless you.

25   And if you wilt make me an altar of stone, you shalt not build it of hewn stone: for if you lift up your tool upon it, you hast polluted it.

26   Neither shalt you go up by steps unto mine altar, that your nakedness be not discovered thereon.

It's amazing that God gave the Israelites a chance to see him from afar. Each and every one of them heard the trumpet of God. They heard the thunders and saw with their eyes things they associated with reasons to fear. Lightning and dark clouds. A voice so loud they could not escape it. As Moses approached God, the people stepped back. They were encouraged to be close to God, to hear Him and Moses speak, but they decided to move away, either because of fear or something else.

It is the initiative of God that has Moses return to them. God calls Moses up the mountain. Then sends him down to talk with the people. It is a message of who God is and what He expects from those who would be His.

God sets himself apart from all the "other would-be gods." He is the only real one. He explains this to the people. Even His altars of worship can not be made by the hands of man. Of man collect the stone, but he cannot put his mark on the stone. An altar of worship to God is to be beauty unto God. Not beauty onto the man who makes it. Think of the things you have put before God. Did you build an altar of brick?

Dear Lord Jesus!

Who am I that You should love me this much? Your kindness and love draw us to you. You are above all. You are truly worthy of our worship. God help me to set You above all else in my life. Your love for us knows no bounds. Your daily provision and much more show how much you care for me. Lord, may I be that beacon of light pointing the way to You—the God who loves man.

In Jesus name, Amen.

DAY #64
EXODUS 21:1-11

1   Now these *are* the judgments which you shalt set before them.
2   If you buy an Hebrew servant, six years he shall serve: and in the seventh he shall go out free for nothing.
3   If he came in by himself, he shall go out by himself: if he were married, then his wife shall go out with him.
4   If his master have given him a wife, and she have born him sons or daughters; the wife and her children shall be her master's, and he shall go out by himself.
5   And if the servant shall plainly say, I love my master, my wife, and my children; I will not go out free:
6   Then his master shall bring him unto the judges; he shall also bring him to the door, or unto the door post; and his master shall bore his ear through with an aul; and he shall serve him for ever.
7   And if a man sell his daughter to be a maidservant, she shall not go out as the menservants do.
8   If she please not her master, who hath betrothed her to himself, then shall he let her be redeemed: to sell her unto a strange nation he shall have no power, seeing he hath dealt deceitfully with her.
9   And if he have betrothed her unto his son, he shall deal with her after the manner of daughters.
10 If he take him another *wife*; her food, her raiment, and her duty of marriage, shall he not diminish.
11 And if he do not these three unto her, then shall she go out free without money.

I find it fascinating that the first thing communicated by God to the Israelites after the Ten Commandments was freeing slaves. These people who were slaves had slaves to themselves. These 12 verses change the concept of slavery from a lifetime into a contractual six years. You agree to work for free for up to six years when you get sold or sell yourself into slavery.

Notice the rules here that protect women. These judgements call into question those who had given servants no choice but to be married to their owners. They call out some truly cruel practices. Still, she can go free at the end of her time – at the end of six years.

Perhaps God was pointing out the irony of a people freed from slavery who have enslaved their own people.

Reading this passage makes you wonder how many slaves were freed that day. People who served more than six years would suddenly be freed. Then there would be those who continued to choose to serve for the rest of their lives.

Dear Lord Jesus,

Help me choose to do the right things versus having to be told what is right. Grant me wisdom that I might make choices that please you when I do not know which answer seems right to You. Enable me to stand against evil. Strengthen me, that I may be bold and stand for Your desires over that of this world's ways. Lord, I also ask that you awaken those around me to this need to stand for what is right. Embolden them also to stand strong if we must stand alone.

In Jesus name, Amen.

DAY #65
EXODUS 21:12-15

12 He that smites a man, so that he die, shall be surely put to death.
13 And if a man lie not in wait, but God deliver *him* into his hand; then I will appoint you a place whither he shall flee.
14 But if a man come presumptuously upon his neighbour, to slay him with guile; you shalt take him from mine altar, that he may die.
15 And he that smites his father, or his mother, shall be surely put to death.

This passage is all about the law regarding the murder. It explains the simplicity of the death penalty. If you disrespect the lives of others, your life gets snuffed out. BUT, should a man die unintentionally at your hand, God will make a safe haven for that person to flee to.

Yet, if a man has guile, evil intent in his heart, and intends to kill someone but is stopped by some means for whatever reason. Even if it is only a verbal threat, they will be exiled. Notice the part here about exile. Exile here is the removal from God's altar. God considers his people gathered in this one area HIS altar. If one is exiled, they do not get manna and do not have the benefits of a God who loves them. They have no provision or protection. A lonesome death of hunger or horror is to come.

The last verse here is on the murder of a parent. Keep in mind God has clear directives for parents. Parents are to give their children what they need to grow. They are to love them. There is no allowance for abuse by parents in any way. They lived in tents as multiple family units. So, the murder of a parent is viewed as especially evil.

Dear Lord Jesus,

Your love expresses a desire to protect the innocent. Lord, your love of the Hebrew people and your just laws established our beliefs that created America. The concept of innocent until proven guilty is all about protecting the innocent. Your law sets the standard. Help me to see how YOU are the one who sets standards. Help me to share that wisdom on how our laws are a reflection of your laws.

In Jesus name, Amen.

DAY #66
EXODUS 21:16-25

16   And he that steals a man, and sells him, or if he be found in his hand, he shall surely be put to death.
17   And he that curses his father, or his mother, shall surely be put to death.
18   And if men strive together, and one smite another with a stone, or with *his* fist, and he die not, but keepeth *his* bed:

19 If he rise again, and walk abroad upon his staff, then shall he that smote *him* be quit: only he shall pay *for* the loss of his time, and shall cause *him* to be thoroughly healed.
20 And if a man smite his servant, or his maid, with a rod, and he die under his hand; he shall be surely punished.
21 Notwithstanding, if he continue a day or two, he shall not be punished: for he *is* his money.
22 If men strive, and hurt a woman with child, so that her fruit depart *from her*, and yet no mischief follow: he shall be surely punished, according as the woman's husband will lay upon him; and he shall pay as the judges *determine*.
23 And if *any* mischief follow, then you shalt give life for life,
24 Eye for eye, tooth for tooth, hand for hand, foot for foot,
25 Burning for burning, wound for wound, stripe for stripe.

Slavery, as it existed in America, resulted from "man-stealing"; they were forcibly taken and forced to be slaves. This is addressed here, and the punishment is death. You have to wonder why no one asked questions about this.

The one crime here that is not in our modern law is the person who curses his parents. When they go through a rebellious stage, most children may get angry with their parents. Cursing parents today is not a crime. This goes back to the commandment of honoring your parents. Something that is a lifelong requirement.

Also shown here is the importance and value of life. The unborn baby is of great importance also. The abuse of a pregnant woman is seen as a great horror that is mentioned alongside the death penalty. Patterns of behavior are also mentioned here. If you think about this concept, we did not discuss it until the last hundred years. Yet this was written thousands of years ago.

The eye for an eye, tooth for a tooth ruling is mentioned here. It causes a bit of wonder how well-known some ancient laws were. It could also mean that some laws were seen as universal. They would exist everywhere.

Dear Lord Jesus,

Help me, Lord, to put you first. Help me to place you above all of my desires. Remove from me my selfishness so that your will is manifest in my life. Lord, help me to be an example of Your love. Your love is far beyond my own. So I need help to do this. Guide me so that I may be that which you desire.

In Jesus name, Amen.

DAY #67
EXODUS 21:26-27

26   And if a man smite the eye of his servant, or the eye of his maid, that it perish; he shall let him go free for his eye's sake.
27   And if he smite out his manservant's tooth, or his maidservant's tooth; he shall let him go free for his tooth's sake.

This establishes that slaves may be property, BUT they must never be harmed in any way. Whatever the cost of a slave, if you assign work that ends up causing them harm, they get to go free.

People sold themselves into slavery to pay debts. They sold their children to pay debts. As shown in an earlier passage in Exodus, they could only be owned for six years. Now it is established that no act of cruelty could be allowed upon a slave.

Our ideas of slavery include acts of cruelty being allowed. This seems closer to what we call servitude, but there is no pay. Unless you consider those who are paying off a debt with their service, these rules regarding slavery make the Israelite community a truly unique and special people. It is another reason to consider how God's chosen people are set apart from the rest of the world by their laws. It also gives us reason to stop and think about how cruelties were allowed when those who owned slaves in the USA had the Bible. They claimed to know it also. Did they skip these sections knowingly?

Dear Lord Jesus,

You are truly the God above all. You take care of the prominent and the slave. You care for us with such love that is beyond our own understanding. Help me to share this wondrous love you have for me and others. Send me that others may hear of your great love.

In Jesus name, Amen.

DAY #68
EXODUS 21:28-36

28 If an ox gore a man or a woman, that they die: then the ox shall be surely stoned, and his flesh shall not be eaten; but the owner of the ox *shall be* quit.
29 But if the ox were wont to push with his horn in time past, and it hath been testified to his owner, and he hath not kept him in, but that he hath killed a man or a woman; the ox shall be stoned, and his owner also shall be put to death.
30 If there be laid on him a sum of money, then he shall give for the ransom of his life whatsoever is laid upon him.
31 Whether he have gored a son, or have gored a daughter, according to this judgment shall it be done unto him.
32 If the ox shall push a manservant or a maidservant; he shall give unto their master thirty shekels of silver, and the ox shall be stoned.
33 And if a man shall open a pit, or if a man shall dig a pit, and not cover it, and an ox or an ass fall therein;
34 The owner of the pit shall make *it* good, *and* give money unto the owner of them; and the dead *beast* shall be his.
35 And if one man's ox hurt another's, that he die; then they shall sell the live ox, and divide the money of it; and the dead *ox* also they shall divide.
36 Or if it be known that the ox hath used to push in time past, and his owner hath not kept him in; he shall surely pay ox for ox; and the dead shall be his own.

How effectively does a guy care for an animal that has the potential to inflict harm on another? How responsible does he act concerning the animal? Does he take action to prevent future troubles? Animals have their own personalities also. That is part of what this says. But what does the owner do when one of these animals starts to do wrong? If he does nothing corrective, something is dangerously wrong. Behavior patterns are important here. They establish who is really in the wrong. God's Word here is about man's ability to take away fear and anger from animals if they are properly cared for. This is not about whether an animal is fed. This type of care is emotional. Shouldn't a person caring for a herd notice the one who is acting differently?

Cruelty to animals is also mentioned here. The pit being dug for various reasons is all about properly caring for animals. They are God's creatures.

In our culture, many see those who are cruel to animals as having a special place in hell made just for them. This passage tells us that we have a responsibility to others and animals to provide care beyond simple provision. We have to do more to ensure the animal is happy and that others are safe.

Dear Lord Jesus,

You created all the animals before you made us. The book of Exodus tells us how much You desire that we care for them and look after them with kindness. You do so much to help us see what is right and what is wrong. Lord, please do not stop prodding us in the right direction. Lord, please use even our care and love of animals as a way to reach others for You!

In Jesus name, Amen.

DAY #69
EXODUS 22:1-15

1 If a man shall steal an ox, or a sheep, and kill it, or sell it; he shall restore five oxen for an ox, and four sheep for a sheep.
2 If a thief be found breaking up, and be smitten that he die, *there shall* no blood *be shed* for him.
3 If the sun be risen upon him, *there shall be* blood *shed* for him; *for* he should make full restitution; if he have nothing, then he shall be sold for his theft.
4 If the theft be certainly found in his hand alive, whether it be ox, or ass, or sheep; he shall restore double.
5 If a man shall cause a field or vineyard to be eaten, and shall put in his beast, and shall feed in another man's field; of the best of his own field, and of the best of his own vineyard, shall he make restitution.
6 If fire break out, and catch in thorns, so that the stacks of corn, or the standing corn, or the field, be consumed *therewith*; he that kindled the fire shall surely make restitution.
7 If a man shall deliver unto his neighbour money or stuff to keep, and it be stolen out of the man's house; if the thief be found, let him pay double.
8 If the thief be not found, then the master of the house shall be brought unto the judges, *to see* whether he have put his hand unto his neighbour's goods.
9 For all manner of trespass, *whether it be* for ox, for ass, for sheep, for raiment, *or* for any manner of lost thing, which *another* challenges to be his, the cause of both parties shall

come before the judges; *and* whom the judges shall condemn, he shall pay double unto his neighbour.
10   If a man deliver unto his neighbour an ass, or an ox, or a sheep, or any beast, to keep; and it die, or be hurt, or driven away, no man seeing *it*:
11   *then* shall an oath of the LORD be between them both, that he hath not put his hand unto his neighbour's goods; and the owner of it shall accept *thereof*, and he shall not make *it* good.
12   And if it be stolen from him, he shall make restitution unto the owner thereof.
13   If it be torn in pieces, *then* let him bring it *for* witness, *and* he shall not make good that which was torn.
14   And if a man borrow *ought* of his neighbour, and it be hurt, or die, the owner thereof *being* not with it, he shall surely make *it* good.
15   *But* if the owner thereof *be* with it, he shall not make *it* good: if it *be* an hired *thing*, it came for his hire.

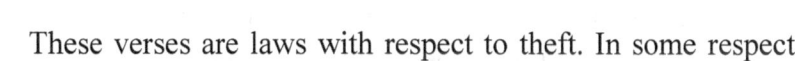

These verses are laws with respect to theft. In some respect, this is a statement that personal property is a right; also, a person's property should not be removed without his/her permission.

Verse 2 here seemed the hardest to understand due to the old English. In truth, this refers to a person breaking up what was stolen or selling what was stolen.

Penalties for doing what is wrong have to hurt. It's one thing to be penalized for something you did accidentally, but quite another to be penalized for something you know you knowingly did wrong. Doubling the price is painful. Think about the laws of today. Do they protect your right to property? Do they hurt those who get caught knowingly stealing?

Dear Lord Jesus,

Our concept of freedom comes from you. Our understanding of the rights that come from you is within each of us. Life, Liberty, and Property are three of those things. They are mentioned after acknowledging You. We were built to put You first in our lives and to give You, Lord Jesus, the honor and glory due to your name.

In Jesus name, Amen.

DAY #70
EXODUS 22:16-20

16   And if a man entice a maid that is not betrothed, and lie with her, he shall surely endow her to be his wife.
17   If her father utterly refuse to give her unto him, he shall pay money according to the dowry of virgins.
18   You shalt not suffer a witch to live.
19   Whosoever lieth with a beast shall surely be put to death.
20   He that sacrifices unto *any* god, save unto the LORD only, he shall be utterly destroyed.

This passage starts with a look at sex before marriage. This verse tells the man if he should propose to her. He should give a true promise of marriage that he will follow through on. But, the father of the maid can say no to this. This is one of the reasons that a man asks permission to marry from the father of the woman he intends to marry. If the man asking is not trusted by the father for various reasons, he can say no and protect his daughter. The man can prove himself better or be the man the maid's father believes.

Verse 18 uses the word "suffer," which was used in old English to mean "allow." Considering this placed between two passages about sexual relations, this is also likely to be a reference to the lesbianism known to occur amongst witches.

Verse 19 is so abhorrent, the fact that it is said is almost self-explanatory. Many have served in our military and have witnessed this and pondered carrying out the sentence.

Verse 20 stands by itself. The punishment of being utterly destroyed is seen later in the scripture. It goes beyond his being put to death. It hints that God will take action.

Dear Lord Jesus,

Your love goes beyond our understanding. You loved us first, even when we were deep in our sins. Lord, you can redeem us from every sin that the law points out. Lord, may you be glorified for Your wondrous love that is beyond our own ability to love deserves our praise. Please, Lord, guide our steps and keep us from seeking our own pleasures. Lord, may you mold us so that our pleasure turns from sin to the joy of worshipping you!

In Jesus' name, Amen.

DAY #71
EXODUS 22:21-28

21 You shalt neither vex a stranger, nor oppress him: for you were strangers in the land of Egypt.
22 You shall not afflict any widow, or fatherless child.
23 If you afflict them in any wise, and they cry at all unto me, I will surely hear their cry;
24 And my wrath shall wax hot, and I will kill you with the sword; and your wives shall be widows, and your children fatherless.
25 If you lend money to *any of* my people *that is* poor by you, you shalt not be to him as an usurer, neither shalt you lay upon him usury.
26 If you at all take your neighbour's raiment to pledge, you shalt deliver it unto him by that the sun goes down:
27 For that *is* his covering only, it *is* his raiment for his skin: wherein shall he sleep? and it shall come to pass, when he cries unto me, that I will hear; for I *am* gracious.
28 You shalt not revile the gods, nor curse the ruler of your people.

This God of love even cares about how His people treat strangers. Of note here is a general acceptance of those who do not know the God of Israel. This is important as it demonstrates that, unlike Islam, Judaism does not expect its laws to be followed by non-Muslims. Instead, the law (Torah) given by God separates those who follow it from others and has done so throughout history. This is backed up by the last verse in this passage.

The importance of how widows and fatherless children are treated separates Judeo-Christian culture from all others. In some cultures, these are the "disposable" ones. The ones to ignore, and the ones who can be treated like dung. By God's reasoning here, if they are treated badly, he will act. There is no punishment for not following this law from God other than an understanding that HE will indeed act against those who treat the widows and fatherless poorly.

God condemns the practice of loaning money to the poor and expecting money back with interest. It's a simple recognition that if they are poor, doing so is beyond their ability. You then become an oppressor of the poor if you do this, so don't do it.

The concept of taking collateral for a promise is also a problem when that collateral is something that can not afford to be lost. Especially if the collateral given is not returned within a day, ensure they have it when needed.

Dear Lord Jesus,

Lord, I ask that you show me how to share this great love You have with others. Your love for the strangers, widows, and the fatherless is like that of a protective father. Lord, help me to share Your Word on these things. Help me share your great love for those who do not know you and how knowing Your Word can improve their lives.

In Jesus name, Amen,

DAY #72
EXODUS 22:29-31

29   You shalt not delay *to offer* the first of your ripe fruits, and of your liquors: the firstborn of your sons shalt you give unto me.
30   Likewise shalt you do with your oxen, *and* with your sheep: seven days it shall be with his dam; on the eighth day you shalt give it me.
31   And you shall be holy men unto me: neither shall you eat *any* flesh *that is* torn of beasts in the field; you shall cast it to the dogs.

When I first heard about the importance of giving the first fruits, I questioned it, but I later thought to put it to the test. I did it. The results were what I would describe as undeniable blessings. I find it sad that I somehow missed this concept until I was over fifty years of age. I ponder now how it is that I missed this in my readings, but God knows the best timing for us to learn things. Today, for those of us whose income is monetary, giving God your tithe before any other expense is all that is needed. Today's ease of electronic transfers makes this truly possible. Unless your payment is in cash, then it's as simple as setting that money aside and putting it on the offering plate.

Verse 31 shouts how different the God of the Jews and Christians is from those of the false ones. Our God wants us to treat those who visit us with such care and love that even those with false gods can be shamed by our love. This does not mean we do not call out evil or recognize false/fake gods and those who lyingly sell them to others. We have a duty to God to do this. But the visiting stranger gets special treatment. Consider it a guideline for friendship evangelism. When you are there for your friend when they need you, your life, your bond as a friend, stands out as an example of God's love for you. How they see you interact with your family and others stands out. Ask yourself if that is what your neighbors see in you today.

Dear Lord Jesus,

Lord, guide me to greater love in You for all your kept promises, such as the greatness in giving the first fruits of our labor. Sometimes like this, you simply tell us this is something we should do, but it is not until we do it that we learn how great it is for us. To you truly belongs all our honor and glory. I ask Lord that you embolden me. Use me to reach those around me with Your love that goes beyond our understanding. Help me, Lord, that I may be such a person that stands for You in everything I do!

In Jesus name, Amen.

DAY #73
EXODUS 23:1-8

1 You shalt not raise a false report: put not your hand with the wicked to be an unrighteous witness.
2 You shalt not follow a multitude to *do* evil; neither shalt you speak in a cause to decline after many to wrest *judgment*:
3 Neither shalt you countenance a poor man in his cause.

4 If you meet thine enemy's ox or his ass going astray, you shalt surely bring it back to him again.

5 If you see the ass of him that hates you lying under his burden, and would forbear to help him, you shalt surely help with him.

6 You shalt not wrest the judgment of your poor in his cause.

7 Keep you far from a false matter; and the innocent and righteous slay you not: for I will not justify the wicked.

8 And you shalt take no gift: for the gift blinds the wise, and perverts the words of the righteous.

Verse 1 is about the importance of truth. There are some who would tear down a man for not believing what they do. That one thing would have them create lies against him until one of them is believed. A man's character creates his legacy. If he is one given to lying or associating with those who do evil, his character cannot be trusted, which will be his legacy. But your own conduct, your own character matters incredibly to God. He wants the best for you. These laws make one stand out for doing what is right, even amid a crowd of those who choose to do wrong.

Verse two speaks of doing what is right even when all around you are doing what is wrong. Can you stand up when something wrong is being said, and you must be present and vote with your feet against the evil by walking out? Standing alone is not bad, especially when you are doing what God wants you to do.

Verses 3 and 6 speak of the awkward truth that a man without financial means often loses in a court based on his financial limitations. As Christ was no respecter of persons, so we must be. We must never oppose someone because they have less money. We should take our stand based on what is true.

Verses 4 and 5 speak of how we should treat an enemy kindly. Notice it says nothing about how we should treat a friend. Why is this? Because if we treat an enemy with kindness, how much better should we treat those whom we count as friends? How could we walk by an animal that has collapsed due to carrying too heavy of a burden and not help him? His master's owner should not matter to us. Just as a man struggling with the burden of the weight of his own sins, we should show the way to Christ.

Verses 7 and 8 speak to being just and acting fairly when you are in a place to pass judgement. Doing what is right and true should not have any questions within you. Add in that no outward influence should be able to sway you. In America, this talks about lobbyists and the wealthy bribing politicians to get them to do what they want. These are also reasons for good men in this country to recuse themselves when assigned positions of authority when they have connections financially that could bring influence to their thoughts.

Dear Lord Jesus,

How we live matters. Your guidance in these things, Your example of how to live while You walked the earth, show us how we ought to live. Lord, let us not forget how glorious and great your promises are to us. Let us put You first and, in so doing, place our behavior in line with Your desires over our own.

In Jesus name, Amen.

DAY #74
EXODUS 23:9-19

9   Also you shalt not oppress a stranger: for you know the heart of a stranger, seeing you were strangers in the land of Egypt.

10   And six years you shalt sow your land, and shalt gather in the fruits thereof:

11   But the seventh *year* you shalt let it rest and lie still; that the poor of your people may eat: and what they leave the beasts of the field shall eat. In like manner you shalt deal with your vineyard, *and* with your oliveyard.

12   Six days you shalt do your work, and on the seventh day you shalt rest: that your ox and your ass may rest, and the son of your handmaid, and the stranger, may be refreshed.

13   And in all *things* that I have said unto you be circumspect: and make no mention of the name of other gods, neither let it be heard out of your mouth.

14   Three times you shalt keep a feast unto me in the year.

15   You shalt keep the feast of unleavened bread: (you shalt eat unleavened bread seven days, as I commanded you, in the time appointed of the month Abib; for in it you came out from Egypt: and none shall appear before me empty:)

16   And the feast of harvest, the first fruits of your labours, which you hast sown in the field: and the feast of ingathering, *which is* in the end of the year, when you hast gathered in your labours out of the field.

17   Three times in the year all your males shall appear before the Lord GOD.

18   You shalt not offer the blood of my sacrifice with leavened bread; neither shall the fat of my sacrifice remain until the morning.

19   The first of the first fruits of your land you shalt bring into the house of the LORD your God. You shalt not seethe a kid in his mother's milk.

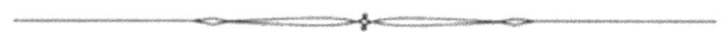

This passage begins with a reminder of who the Israelite people are; they are redeemed slaves, saved by God Almighty. They were living as strangers in a strange land.

Next, the importance of the seventh year, the year we know as the year of Jubilee, is addressed. A year of rest for the land. If you think about it, this is the type of field that would be the way the poor get fed. Scientifically, you can read about the importance of a field receiving rest.

The importance of a six-day work week and a day of rest to follow also hits. Rest is important. Recreation is important. We need to understand that God loves us so much he had to make it a rule for us to begin to recognize how unhealthy it is for us to work seven days a week.

The next verse refers to not even mentioning the other "gods," whose make-believe existence was created by men. This would give them a reason to be remembered. This was an exclusive community. If a conversation about these make-believe entities were forbidden, they would be forgotten. Remember, God did say he is a jealous God.

Then the three times for the men to appear before God. These are the three feasts. While we are not Jewish and do not celebrate their festivals, think of it as three holidays. What three holidays stand out to you? Christmas, Easter, and Thanksgiving are three times families gather and celebrate God in the United States.

This passage ends with an emphasis on giving God the first fruits of your labor. When preachers talk about tithing, not enough of them talk about this also. There is a great blessing when you tithe.

But when you give the first fruits. There is an additional blessing when you pay your tithe before making any other expenses from that amount. Most may never understand this because they never attempt to do this. But I say to you, as one who never ceases to be amazed by this blessing, you should try this!

Dear Lord Jesus,

How is your love so wonderful that you do so much for us. You even made rules for us so that we might better know you and follow your will. Lord, help us see the importance of seeking the desires of Your heart and our own. Let us place you above all in our lives. Lord, may our lives be a reflection of Your great love so that others may know and love you.

In Jesus name, Amen.

DAY #75
EXODUS 23:20-33

20   Behold, I send an Angel before you, to keep you in the way, and to bring you into the place which I have prepared.
21   Beware of him, and obey his voice, provoke him not; for he will not pardon your transgressions: for my name *is* in him.
22   But if you shalt indeed obey his voice, and do all that I speak; then I will be an enemy unto your enemies, and an adversary unto your adversaries.

23 For mine Angel shall go before you, and bring you in unto the Amorites, and the Hittites, and the Perizzites, and the Canaanites, the Hivites, and the Jebusites: and I will cut them off.

24 You shalt not bow down to their gods, nor serve them, nor do after their works: but you shalt utterly overthrow them, and quite break down their images.

25 And you shall serve the LORD your God, and he shall bless your bread, and your water; and I will take sickness away from the midst of you.

26 There shall nothing cast their young, nor be barren, in your land: the number of your days I will fulfil.

27 I will send my fear before you, and will destroy all the people to whom you shalt come, and I will make all your enemies turn their backs unto you.

28 And I will send hornets before you, which shall drive out the Hivite, the Canaanite, and the Hittite, from before you.

29 I will not drive them out from before you in one year; lest the land become desolate, and the beast of the field multiply against you.

30 By little and little I will drive them out from before you, until you be increased, and inherit the land.

31 And I will set your bounds from the Red sea even unto the sea of the Philistines, and from the desert unto the river: for I will deliver the inhabitants of the land into your hand; and you shalt drive them out before you.

32 You shalt make no covenant with them, nor with their gods.

33 They shall not dwell in your land, lest they make you sin against me: for if you serve their gods, it will surely be a snare unto you.

These first few verses hint at the concept of the United One that is given in Deuteronomy 6:4. A messenger in whom is the name of God. Angel literally means messenger and is used to attempt to define God's messengers. In this case, the messenger can be seen as a fiery pillar or as a pillar of cloud.

Can you imagine the comfort that would come from not having to think about where you are going? You only have to follow the pillar that leads the way. Jeremiah 10:23 says, "O LORD, I know that the way of man *is* not in himself: *it is* not in man that walketh to direct his steps." How much more so to those who learn day and night to direct their steps to follow the movement of God?

This gets even better; God makes promises to those who follow Him. He offers huge benefits and, at the same time, promises some hardship ahead. He tells of coming confrontations that HE will take care of. Maybe this is to tell the men to be good stewards and protectors to arm and prepare themselves for coming battles. But these battles will not be terrible, for HE goes before them, bringing terrible fear and things that will drive many from the lands they are entering.

There are clues here warning of serious problems if they do not listen. All they have to do is obey. Sounds simple enough. Make no treaties; do not allow those with the false gods to stay in the land, for they will corrupt you. How hard are these two requests? Consider the benefits of simple obedience. For those who serve as defenders, aka in their army, it means endless victories. If you were one of the armies, would you not be screaming YES! WE WILL FOLLOW YOU! Think about the battles you would enter with such confidence that God is with you. Promised battles with promised victories.

Dear Lord Jesus,

Direct my steps. I know I am foolish and do not always desire to do that which is right. Lord, guide my steps; put my feet on the right path. I want to take part in victories for YOU! I want to brag about having endured and seen Your work clearing the battlefield as a mighty warrior had won the victory that I participated in. Lord, use me in this battle to share your Word, to bring the message of HOPE to the loss of Your great love. May my words and actions be counted as those which led men and women to Your love. May they be known for drawing the lost to You. May YOU be glorified in this battle, YOU have already won!

In Jesus name, Amen.

DAY #76
EXODUS 24:1-11

1 And he said unto Moses, Come up unto the LORD, you, and Aaron, Nadab, and Abihu, and seventy of the elders of Israel; and worship you afar off.
2 And Moses alone shall come near the LORD: but they shall not come nigh; neither shall the people go up with him.
3 And Moses came and told the people all the words of the LORD, and all the judgments: and all the people answered with one voice, and said, All the words which the LORD hath said will we do.
4 And Moses wrote all the words of the LORD, and rose up early in the morning, and built an altar under the hill, and twelve pillars, according to the twelve tribes of Israel.

5	And he sent young men of the children of Israel, which offered burnt offerings, and sacrificed peace offerings of oxen unto the LORD.
6	And Moses took half of the blood, and put *it* in basons; and half of the blood he sprinkled on the altar.
7	And he took the book of the covenant, and read in the audience of the people: and they said, All that the LORD has said will we do, and be obedient.
8	And Moses took the blood, and sprinkled *it* on the people, and said, Behold the blood of the covenant, which the LORD hath made with you concerning all these words.
9	Then went up Moses, and Aaron, Nadab, and Abihu, and seventy of the elders of Israel:
10	And they saw the God of Israel: and *there was* under his feet as it were a paved work of a sapphire stone, and as it were the body of heaven in *his* clearness.
11	And upon the nobles of the children of Israel he laid not his hand: also they saw God, and did eat and drink.

Can you imagine being one of Israel's leaders and hearing that Moses is handpicking some of you to join him in approaching God? Then you learn it is not some. It's all of you! Would you be quaking in your boots? Would you be scared, glad, overjoyed, excited, and all of it over and over?

It's not unusual for leaders to be older men. This may be why there is mention that those younger leaders of the twelve tribes did the sacrificing. This was not an easy job for an older man. It stood out that only the younger men did this. Even though they were a minority of the men present.

Then they moved upward, and they saw Elohim, the one and only God. Moses and the seventy-three leaders of Israel see God, and how do they describe Him?

> And they saw the God of Israel: and *there was* under his feet as it were a paved work of a sapphire stone, and as it were the body of heaven in *his* clearness.

When you think about this description, what does it say about how God appeared to them? They were in the presence of God, and the unusual thing to them was that where God's feet were over, a jewelled path appeared. Did God appear as a man to them? Was he so normal-looking that there was nothing at all that stood out and set him apart? Would that mean that this appearance is what we call a pre-incarnate image of Christ? Was this Jesus, who was not supposed to have anything in his physical appearance that made men take notice? These men saw God and were not nervous. They did things they normally would like to eat and drink. They had no fear in His presence. Maybe they were in such awe and had no words to describe the God they saw. But this paints a picture of an approachable God, a God who cares.

Dear Lord Jesus,

How is it that you love us so that you make it possible for us to approach you.? This loving-kindness, this desire to care for everything about us despite our sinful and ignorant nature amazes me. Lord, may you use me to share your incredible love for us. Use me that I may speak of Your great love to others.

In Jesus name, Amen.

DAY #77
EXODUS 24:12-18

12   And the LORD said unto Moses, Come up to me into the mount, and be there: and I will give you tables of stone, and a law, and commandments which I have written; that you mayest teach them.
13   And Moses rose up, and his minister Joshua: and Moses went up into the mount of God.
14   And he said unto the elders, Tarry you here for us, until we come again unto you: and, behold, Aaron and Hur *are* with you: if any man have any matters to do, let him come unto them.
15   And Moses went up into the mount, and a cloud covered the mount.
16   And the glory of the LORD abode upon mount Sinai, and the cloud covered it six days: and the seventh day he called unto Moses out of the midst of the cloud.
17   And the sight of the glory of the LORD *was* like devouring fire on the top of the mount in the eyes of the children of Israel.
18   And Moses went into the midst of the cloud, and gat him up into the mount: and Moses was in the mount forty days and forty nights.

There are a few things here that should stand out. Joshua was one of Moses' servants, and he traveled with him. God also had set aside the elders to see HIM personally. They saw and knew GOD in person. They ate and drank in the presence of God. But no comment is made about preparing to go on a journey or preparing to be away for a while. Where did the food come from? Did they bring it with them, or did God prepare it?

If God prepared the food for them, they must have never questioned if Moses was OKAY for most of the forty days and nights. After all, if God provided such things while they were in the presence of God, how much more so would he provide for Moses and Joshua? But what would you think after forty days of your leader being absent? When people went asking for Moses, can you imagine being one of those called and asked where Moses is if you were one of the seventy-two leaders Moses entrusted? Wait—it's not Moses who entrusted you with the leadership, it's God HIMSELF! What would you say every day to the people when they asked where Moses is?

Maybe you would say, "Moses is on the mountain with God. God is so…" as you get this smile of satisfaction as you think of the God you saw. You continue, "He is so…so …. Well, God is taking care of Moses, don't worry." Even after twenty days, would your response change? After thirty days?

Here you are with a people whose daily food is provided miraculously. The food on the mountain was likely provided in the same manner to them. So they should not have wondered if he had enough food at all. Forty days…, would you begin to question what you and all the other elders of Israel had seen? Would you begin to question what happened to your leader? Had this God who provided for your daily needs after delivering ALL of you from slavery done something awful to Moses, your leader? W-a-i-t, Moses was God's chosen leader. You also had to have talked with Aaron, who said Moses survived alone in a desert for a long time. If Moses survived that...

Dear Lord Jesus,

    I am not asking for a mountain-top experience with You. You provide for me each day; even though I sometimes struggle to acknowledge how you do this for me, I know you are my provider. Lord, I know you care for me. I know You alone are worthy of my praise, for you plan ahead to meet my needs even before I know of them. Lord, help me that I may do that which you desire. Help me that I may be one who seeks after Your desires first. Then Lord, use me to share Your great love, for it is abundant.

In Jesus name, Amen.

DAY #78
EXODUS 25:1-7

1   And the LORD spake unto Moses, saying,
2   Speak unto the children of Israel, that they bring me an offering: of every man that giveth it willingly with his heart you shall take my offering.
3   And this *is* the offering which you shall take of them; gold, and silver, and brass,
4   And blue, and purple, and scarlet, and fine linen, and goats' *hair*,
5   And rams' skins dyed red, and badgers' skins, and shittim wood,
6   Oil for the light, spices for anointing oil, and for sweet incense,
7   Onyx stones, and stones to be set in the ephod, and in the breastplate.

God is asking for an offering of what many of us consider to be luxuries that we would not expect of migrants, even in large numbers. That would mean that they have such valuables that had to come from their past Egyptian masters. Now there was a purpose, for the Egyptians had given their slaves gifts of valuables as they left.

But God is not demanding these gifts. He said, "of every man that giveth it willingly with his heart, you shall take my offering." That is the one thing that truly stands out in contradiction to many other religions at the time. In many ways, it is the difference between a gift and a tax. Each person would give of his/her heart. Giving of themselves, not being forced to give or told to give, is a big difference. This God who delivered them only asks for their choice to give. If you do not want to, that is ok. It is God's job to convince you, not man's.

Dear Lord Jesus,

Help me to see how you continue to provide in so many ways and surprises long before I even know my need. Lord God, show me and create in me the heart of a cheerful giver. Lord, use my gifts, my talents, and more. They are yours.

In Jesus name, Amen.

DAY #79
EXODUS 25:8-40

8. And let them make me a sanctuary; that I may dwell among them.
9. According to all that I shew you, *after* the pattern of the tabernacle, and the pattern of all the instruments thereof, even so shall you make *it*.
10. And they shall make an ark *of* shittim wood: two cubits and a half *shall be* the length thereof, and a cubit and a half the breadth thereof, and a cubit and a half the height thereof.
11. And you shalt overlay it with pure gold, within and without shalt you overlay it, and shalt make upon it a crown of gold round about.
12. And you shalt cast four rings of gold for it, and put *them* in the four corners thereof; and two rings *shall be* in the one side of it, and two rings in the other side of it.
13. And you shalt make staves *of* shittim wood, and overlay them with gold.
14. And you shalt put the staves into the rings by the sides of the ark, that the ark may be borne with them.
15. The staves shall be in the rings of the ark: they shall not be taken from it.
16. And you shalt put into the ark the testimony which I shall give you.
17. And you shalt make a mercy seat *of* pure gold: two cubits and a half *shall be* the length thereof, and a cubit and a half the breadth thereof.
18. And you shalt make two cherubims *of* gold, *of* beaten work shalt you make them, in the two ends of the mercy seat.
19. And make one cherub on the one end, and the other cherub on the other end: *even* of the mercy seat shall you make the cherubims on the two ends thereof.

20 And the cherubims shall stretch forth *their* wings on high, covering the mercy seat with their wings, and their faces *shall look* one to another; toward the mercy seat shall the faces of the cherubims be.

21 And you shalt put the mercy seat above upon the ark; and in the ark you shalt put the testimony that I shall give you.

22 And there I will meet with you, and I will commune with you from above the mercy seat, from between the two cherubims which *are* upon the ark of the testimony, of all *things* which I will give you in commandment unto the children of Israel.

23 You shalt also make a table *of* shittim wood: two cubits *shall be* the length thereof, and a cubit the breadth thereof, and a cubit and a half the height thereof.

24 And you shalt overlay it with pure gold, and make thereto a crown of gold round about.

25 And you shalt make unto it a border of an hand breadth round about, and you shalt make a golden crown to the border thereof round about.

26 And you shalt make for it four rings of gold, and put the rings in the four corners that *are* on the four feet thereof.

27 Over against the border shall the rings be for places of the staves to bear the table.

28 And you shalt make the staves *of* shittim wood, and overlay them with gold, that the table may be borne with them.

29 And you shalt make the dishes thereof, and spoons thereof, and covers thereof, and bowls thereof, to cover withal: *of* pure gold shalt you make them.

30 And you shalt set upon the table shewbread before me alway.

31 And you shalt make a candlestick *of* pure gold: *of* beaten work shall the candlestick be made: his shaft, and his

	branches, his bowls, his knops, and his flowers, shall be of the same.
32	And six branches shall come out of the sides of it; three branches of the candlestick out of the one side, and three branches of the candlestick out of the other side:
33	Three bowls made like unto almonds, *with* a knop and a flower in one branch; and three bowls made like almonds in the other branch, *with* a knop and a flower: so in the six branches that come out of the candlestick.
34	And in the candlestick *shall be* four bowls made like unto almonds, *with* their knops and their flowers.
35	And *there shall be* a knop under two branches of the same, and a knop under two branches of the same, and a knop under two branches of the same, according to the six branches that proceed out of the candlestick.
36	Their knops and their branches shall be of the same: all it *shall be* one beaten work *of* pure gold.
37	And you shalt make the seven lamps thereof: and they shall light the lamps thereof, that they may give light over against it.
38	And the tongs thereof, and the snuff-dishes thereof, *shall be of* pure gold.
39	*of* a talent of pure gold shall he make it, with all these vessels.
40	And look that you make *them* after their pattern, which was shewed you in the mount.

These directions to build a tabernacle, a place of worship, and a seat/place for God to "sit" represent a choice of God to be present with the Israelites. Present is something he has always been, but now it will be noticeable. Now it will be possible to be in the presence of God for most every Israelite.

Dear Lord Jesus,

You first loved us. How true that it is throughout Your Word. How true it is in the World around us. We have a God who loves us so that he removes his "otherness" and puts himself on the cross for our sins. Lord, I praise you and thank you for Your great Love. Help me that I may show others this by how I live and my choice of words.

In Jesus name, Amen.

DAY #80
EXODUS 26:1-14

1 Moreover you shalt make the tabernacle *with* ten curtains *of* fine twined linen, and blue, and purple, and scarlet: *with* cherubims of cunning work shalt you make them.
2 The length of one curtain *shall be* eight and twenty cubits, and the breadth of one curtain four cubits: and every one of the curtains shall have one measure.
3 The five curtains shall be coupled together one to another; and *other* five curtains *shall be* coupled one to another.
4 And you shalt make loops of blue upon the edge of the one curtain from the selvedge in the coupling; and likewise

shalt you make in the uttermost edge of *another* curtain, in the coupling of the second.

5 Fifty loops shalt you make in the one curtain, and fifty loops shalt you make in the edge of the curtain that *is* in the coupling of the second; that the loops may take hold one of another.

6 And you shalt make fifty taches of gold, and couple the curtains together with the taches: and it shall be one tabernacle.

7 And you shalt make curtains *of* goats' *hair* to be a covering upon the tabernacle: eleven curtains shalt you make.

8 The length of one curtain *shall be* thirty cubits, and the breadth of one curtain four cubits: and the eleven curtains *shall be all* of one measure.

9 And you shalt couple five curtains by themselves, and six curtains by themselves, and shalt double the sixth curtain in the forefront of the tabernacle.

10 And you shalt make fifty loops on the edge of the one curtain *that is* outmost in the coupling, and fifty loops in the edge of the curtain which couples the second.

11 And you shalt make fifty taches of brass, and put the taches into the loops, and couple the tent together, that it may be one.

12 And the remnant that remains of the curtains of the tent, the half curtain that remains, shall hang over the backside of the tabernacle.

13 And a cubit on the one side, and a cubit on the other side of that which remains in the length of the curtains of the tent, it shall hang over the sides of the tabernacle on this side and on that side, to cover it.

14 And you shalt make a covering for the tent *of* rams' skins dyed red, and a covering above *of* badgers' skins.

When you read the first verse, you marvel at the beauty, thinking about how blue, purple, and scarlet with the artistic design of cherubims must look. It made me wonder how pretty and wonderous that must have been to see. Yet as you read on, you learn that this beauty was hidden by 3 more layers!

Goat's hair – to some, this sounds ugly in comparison, but it adds a layer of warmth. Add on the ram's dyed red skin you start to see something else. The beauty of Christ and his incredible love for us being inside. The ram's skin covering reminds us of His blood shed for our sins on the cross so that we might have a way out of their penalty due to us through the costly act of believing in HIM. Add on the third outer layer of the badger's skin, which is fairly bland, nondescript, and lacking in beauty. J. Vernon McGee tells us that this is how the world sees Christ. The world does not see His beauty, nor does it see His shed blood for us. Somehow the world passes by it easily.

If you were passing by the Israelites, this tent could appear to be the least valuable. Nevertheless, on the inside, it had to be one of the warmest, safest, and the most awesome in the beauty of any place. Being in the presence of God – the LIVING GOD! Not some fabricated idol had to give you a sense of fear and a desire to present yourself as pure as you can. It also had to make you feel comfortable, secure, and protected from whatever the world could hurl at you. Nothing else mattered from within this realm of beauty but your relationship with God.

Ask yourself how that relationship is today. Are you doing what Christ wants? Are you where He wants you? Are you the good example that Jesus desires you to be?

Dear Lord Jesus,

Mold me and make me after your will. I want to be the one who does what you desire. Lord, help me to seek after Your will. Help me to be the one who shares Your great love. Lord, please do not let me be silent; let me be more than present. Let me be that voice that expresses Your love in everything I do.

In Jesus name, Amen.

DAY #81
EXODUS 26:15-30

16   Ten cubits *shall be* the length of a board, and a cubit and a half *shall be* the breadth of one board.

17   Two tenons *shall there be* in one board, set in order one against another: thus shalt you make for all the boards of the tabernacle.

18   And you shalt make the boards for the tabernacle, twenty boards on the south side southward.

19   And you shalt make forty sockets of silver under the twenty boards; two sockets under one board for his two tenons, and two sockets under another board for his two tenons.

20   And for the second side of the tabernacle on the north side *there shall be* twenty boards:

21   And their forty sockets *of* silver; two sockets under one board, and two sockets under another board.

22   And for the sides of the tabernacle westward you shalt make six boards.

23   And two boards shalt you make for the corners of the tabernacle in the two sides.

24   And they shall be coupled together beneath, and they shall be coupled together above the head of it unto one ring: thus shall it be for them both; they shall be for the two corners.

25   And they shall be eight boards, and their sockets *of* silver, sixteen sockets; two sockets under one board, and two sockets under another board.

26   And you shalt make bars *of* shittim wood; five for the boards of the one side of the tabernacle,

27   And five bars for the boards of the other side of the tabernacle, and five bars for the boards of the side of the tabernacle, for the two sides westward.

28   And the middle bar in the midst of the boards shall reach from end to end.

29   And you shalt overlay the boards with gold, and make their rings *of* gold *for* places for the bars: and you shalt overlay the bars with gold.

30   And you shalt rear up the tabernacle according to the fashion thereof which was shewed you in the mount.

These boards, their socket, and the rods mentioned above construct make the walls for what is called the Tabernacle of God, which Scripture calls the House of God. Some might think of how drab and boring this section appears. Maybe only those interested in construction would have their interest peaked here. BUT there is so much here to tell us about God that should make us wake up and pay special attention. We know it only took one chapter for God to describe the creation of the earth. But the creation of the Tabernacle of God takes much more. Why do we need to ask why that is true? Why did God find it important to communicate so many details on this? Then we need to think that if God found this important, it should be important to us.

This is a movable "house," so every detail had to be provided so that everything was understood and their placement was guaranteed after each move.

Every detail tells us of God's relationship to man before Christ's sacrifice for our sins and after. Even the colors mentioned in the last reading speak out. Blue speaks of the heavens. Red as Christ's blood shed for us. Purple is a blending of those two colors. A statement of royalty and greatness of our God.

To get a poster on this, I recommend going to this site: https://visualtheology.church/products/tabernacle-blueprint

---

Dear Lord Jesus,

Lord, I ask that you help me look at the details here and begin to grasp their importance in communicating who you are and what they tell us about your love for us. Lord, build me up in Your Word so I may become closer to you than ever. Help me to see what I have not seen before. Also, Lord, that You find a way for me to share the knowledge I gain thanks to your loving kindness.

In Jesus name, Amen.

DAY #82
EXODUS 26:31-37

31 And you shalt make a vail *of* blue, and purple, and scarlet, and fine twined linen of cunning work: with cherubims shall it be made:
32 And you shalt hang it upon four pillars of shittim *wood* overlaid with gold: their hooks *shall be of* gold, upon the four sockets of silver.
33 And you shalt hang up the vail under the taches, that you mayest bring in thither within the vail the ark of the testimony: and the vail shall divide unto you between the holy *place* and the most holy.
34 And you shalt put the mercy seat upon the ark of the testimony in the most holy *place*.
35 And you shalt set the table without the vail, and the candlestick over against the table on the side of the tabernacle toward the south: and you shalt put the table on the north side.
36 And you shalt make an hanging for the door of the tent, *of* blue, and purple, and scarlet, and fine twined linen, wrought with needlework.
37 And you shalt make for the hanging five pillars *of* shittim *wood*, and overlay them with gold, *and* their hooks *shall be of* gold: and you shalt cast five sockets of brass for them.

If God feels the details are important, let's look at them. The veil here separated the room inside into two rooms. The larger room became the Holy Place. The smaller room becomes the Most Holy Place. David Guzik wrote that the veil was described by ancient Jews as being four fingers thick so that no one could see inside.

When Christ dies on the cross for our sins, the veil is torn into two. This changes things a bit when we think about a piece of fabric being torn. It was no simple matter that this was done. To the Jews, the tearing of the veil may have made them feel God was becoming unapproachable. They feared entering the Most Holy Place. They had High Priests enter and drop dead because of the sin in their lives. So they added the tradition of the priest putting the end of a rope around himself so he could be pulled out if he died. Would you be fearful of having the task of entering the Most Holy Place?

But the veil being torn means much more for us, the believers in Christ Jesus. It means we all have access to God. It opened the barrier separating God and man BECAUSE Christ died for our sins. His sacrificial love washes white the stain of our sins so that we all may approach God whenever we want. Before the veil was torn, it was only done once a year by only the High Priest.

This thick veil of blue, purple, and scarlet was a barrier to protect the people. Only Christ's atoning blood given so that we may live life eternally was worthy to do this.

Dear Lord Jesus,

You are the lover of my soul. You alone are worthy of my worship. You plan for the impossible for me. You made it possible for my words to reach your ears. Lord, I thank and praise you for this great love you have for me. Use me, God, that I may be one who shares your great love with others.

In Jesus name, Amen

DAY #83
EXODUS 27:1-8

1 And you shalt make an altar *of* shittim wood, five cubits long, and five cubits broad; the altar shall be foursquare: and the height thereof *shall be* three cubits.
2 And you shalt make the horns of it upon the four corners thereof: his horns shall be of the same: and you shalt overlay it with brass.
3 And you shalt make his pans to receive his ashes, and his shovels, and his basons, and his fleshhooks, and his firepans: all the vessels thereof you shalt make *of* brass.
4 And you shalt make for it a grate of network *of* brass; and upon the net shalt you make four brasen rings in the four corners thereof.
5 And you shalt put it under the compass of the altar beneath, that the net may be even to the midst of the altar.
6 And you shalt make staves for the altar, staves *of* shittim wood, and overlay them with brass.
7 And the staves shall be put into the rings, and the staves shall be upon the two sides of the altar, to bear it.
8 Hollow with boards shalt you make it: as it was shewed you in the mount, so shall they make *it*.

Notice that the altar and all that goes with it are not inside the Holy Place. They are outside. This is because man cannot approach God without a substitute to receive the punishment for his son. This is the sacrifice for sin. You have no chance of approaching

God without this. Jesus is the lamb that was slain for our sins. He is GOD and was without stain or blemish because he was without sin. His perfect sacrifice made it possible for us to approach God. His death once and for all our sins made it possible for us to become HIS adopted brethren.

Sin separates us from God. It creates a barrier that only God can bridge. God loved us even when we were covered in the filth of our sins, so much so that He sent His Son to die for us that we might have that reward that comes with having been covered with the sacrificial blood of the Lamb of God, that takes away the sins of the world.

Dear Lord Jesus,

Your love for us knows no bounds. It stands supreme in Your planning for good things so that we may begin to grasp what You have done for us through Your sacrifice on the cross. Lord, may we never fail to grasp your great love for us. Please, Lord Jesus, use me so that I may share your great love with others.

In Jesus' name, Amen.

DAY #84
EXODUS 27:9-21

9 And you shalt make the court of the tabernacle: for the south side southward *there shall be* hangings for the court *of* fine twined linen of an hundred cubits long for one side:

10   And the twenty pillars thereof and their twenty sockets *shall be of* brass; the hooks of the pillars and their fillets *shall be of* silver.

11   And likewise for the north side in length *there shall be* hangings of an hundred *cubits* long, and his twenty pillars and their twenty sockets *of* brass; the hooks of the pillars and their fillets *of* silver.

12   And *for* the breadth of the court on the west side *shall be* hangings of fifty cubits: their pillars ten, and their sockets ten.

13   And the breadth of the court on the east side eastward *shall be* fifty cubits.

14   The hangings of one side *of the gate shall be* fifteen cubits: their pillars three, and their sockets three.

15   And on the other side *shall be* hangings fifteen *cubits*: their pillars three, and their sockets three.

16   And for the gate of the court *shall be* an hanging of twenty cubits, *of* blue, and purple, and scarlet, and fine twined linen, wrought with needlework: *and* their pillars *shall be* four, and their sockets four.

17   All the pillars round about the court *shall be* filleted with silver; their hooks *shall be of* silver, and their sockets *of* brass.

18   The length of the court *shall be* an hundred cubits, and the breadth fifty every where, and the height five cubits *of* fine twined linen, and their sockets *of* brass.

19   All the vessels of the tabernacle in all the service thereof, and all the pins thereof, and all the pins of the court, *shall be of* brass.

20   And you shalt command the children of Israel, that they bring you pure oil olive beaten for the light, to cause the lamp to burn always.

21   In the tabernacle of the congregation without the vail, which *is* before the testimony, Aaron and his sons shall order it from evening to morning before the LORD: *it shall be* a statute for ever unto their generations on the behalf of the children of Israel.

This describes the courtyard area outside of the Holy Place. This area is a type of church. King David said, "Enter into his gates with thanksgiving, *and* into his courts with praise: be thankful unto him *and* bless his name" (Psa 100:4).

Many people might be sombre and think of the debt they owe God when they enter the place where sacrifices are made to take the penalty for their sins. David had a heart after God. He saw that entering the court was entering HIS presence. It should be done with praise and thanksgiving. After all, God brought you to this place. A place of recognition that you have sinned, BUT then he gives you a chance to have your sins paid for. You offer a substitute for your sins. BUT it is accepted by GOD! Is that not a reason to praise His name? Does this not sound like church?

The fine linens that provided the border of the court also have meanings that we need to think about. Rev. 19:8 says, "And to her was granted that she should be arrayed in fine linen, clean and white: for the fine linen is the righteousness of saints." The "her" is the church. We are described with garments that are "washed white as snow" by the "blood of the LAMB." Do you see how David had it right? We should be singing and dancing to HIS praises for what he has done for us!

Dear Lord Jesus,

I thank and praise You for You first loved us. We were stained with the filthiness of our sins, and yet your love did not allow us to wallow in the mire of its despair. You came and died for us, showing us. Your love knows no bounds. Lord, use me! Use me so that I may share your wondrous love with others.

In Jesus name, Amen.

DAY #85
EXODUS 28:1-5

1. And take you unto you Aaron your brother, and his sons with him, from among the children of Israel, that he may minister unto me in the priest's office, *even* Aaron, Nadab and Abihu, Eleazar and Ithamar, Aaron's sons.
2. And you shalt make holy garments for Aaron your brother for glory and for beauty.
3. And you shalt speak unto all *that are* wise hearted, whom I have filled with the spirit of wisdom, that they may make Aaron's garments to consecrate him, that he may minister unto me in the priest's office.
4. And these *are* the garments which they shall make; a breastplate, and an ephod, and a robe, and a broidered coat, a mitre, and a girdle: and they shall make holy garments for Aaron your brother, and his sons, that he may minister unto me in the priest's office.
5. And they shall take gold, and blue, and purple, and scarlet, and fine linen.

Some may say, "this section is not interesting at all." "It's boring." "Not a thing of interest here." BUT we have to think about the details, their meaning and what they are meant to teach us.

This chapter starts with the setting aside of the "Aaronic priesthood." Up to this point, Moses and his brother served in this fashion. It seems to be God pointing out that being a political leader can be too busy to also be a religious leader. Thus separation also sets the Jewish people apart in their culture from many others. Who had priest-kings? Rulers were the ones set up in finery. But in God's eyes, the high priest was to be decked out in splendor. Holy garments! Each of the details in these garments will speak to the personage of Christ.

Dear Lord Jesus,

Thank you for loving me and treating me like I am special in your eyes. You answer my prayers sometimes, even before I know I have a need. Lord, I may not know what tomorrow brings, but it will be spent with You, which is enough. Lord, use me to show others this love You have for us. Lord, help me be Your point man to share the blessings in Your Word.

In Jesus name, Amen.

DAY #86
EXODUS 28:6-14

6   And they shall make the ephod *of* gold, *of* blue, and *of* purple, *of* scarlet, and fine twined linen, with cunning work.

7   It shall have the two shoulder pieces thereof joined at the two edges thereof; and *so* it shall be joined together.

8   And the curious girdle of the ephod, which *is* upon it, shall be of the same, according to the work thereof; *even of* gold, *of* blue, and purple, and scarlet, and fine twined linen.

9   And you shalt take two onyx stones, and grave on them the names of the children of Israel:

10   Six of their names on one stone, and *the other* six names of the rest on the other stone, according to their birth.

11   With the work of an engraver in stone, *like* the engravings of a signet, shalt you engrave the two stones with the names of the children of Israel: you shalt make them to be set in ouches of gold.

12   And you shalt put the two stones upon the shoulders of the ephod *for* stones of memorial unto the children of Israel: and Aaron shall bear their names before the LORD upon his two shoulders for a memorial.

13   And you shalt make ouches *of* gold;

14   And two chains *of* pure gold at the ends; *of* wreathen work shalt you make them, and fasten the wreathen chains to the ouches.

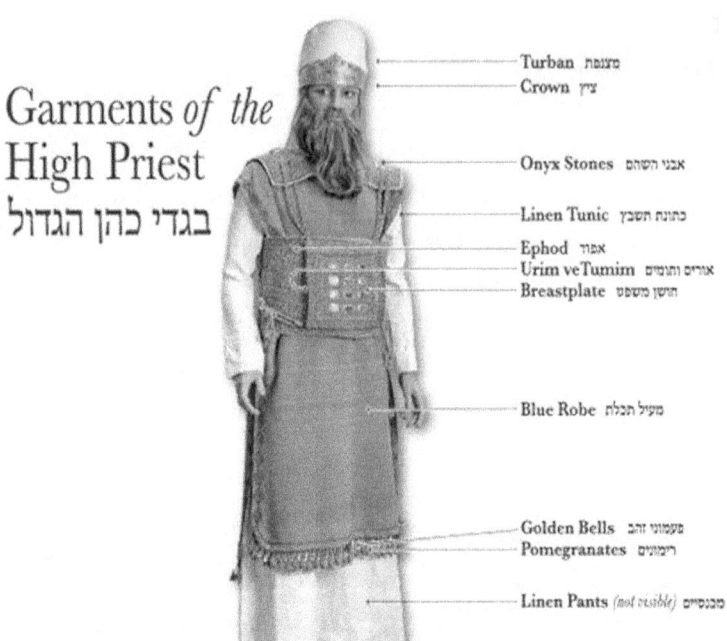

Perhaps the thing that stands out the most here is the onyx stones bearing the names of the tribes of Israel. These stones are symbolic of power and salvation. The high priest carries the weight of Israel on his shoulders. This is the outer garment the high priest wore. In Revelation 1:13, Jesus is seen in a vision as OUR high priest:

> And in the midst of the seven candlesticks [one] like unto the Son of man, clothed with a garment down to the foot, **and girt about the paps with a golden girdle.**

Isaiah describes the girdle as being "righteousness." Paul wrote to the Ephesians about Spiritual Armor. This is something we should wear daily. Ephesians 6:14 says, "Stand, therefore, having your loins girt about with truth…."

Isaiah 9:6 speaks of the government being upon the shoulders of Christ. He is OUR advocate. He is the one who has washed us in his saving blood so that we might have salvation.

Dear Lord Jesus,

You alone are worthy of our praise. You died that we might have life. You advocate for us. You seek what is good for us before we even have an understanding of the need. Lord, help me to share this love beyond my understanding. Help me show others that Your great love is important to them.

In Jesus name, Amen.

DAY #87
EXODUS 28:15-30

15   And you shalt make the breastplate of judgment with cunning work; after the work of the ephod you shalt make it; *of* gold, *of* blue, and *of* purple, and *of* scarlet, and *of* fine twined linen, shalt you make it.
16   Foursquare it shall be *being* doubled; a span *shall be* the length thereof, and a span *shall be* the breadth thereof.
17   And you shalt set in it settings of stones, *even* four rows of stones: [the first] row *shall be* a sardius, a topaz, and a carbuncle: *This shall be* the first row.
18   And the second row *shall be* an emerald, a sapphire, and a diamond.

19 And the third row a ligure, an agate, and an amethyst.

20 And the fourth row a beryl, and an onyx, and a jasper: they shall be set in gold in their inclosings.

21 And the stones shall be with the names of the children of Israel, twelve, according to their names, *like* the engravings of a signet; every one with his name shall they be according to the twelve tribes.

22 And you shalt make upon the breastplate chains at the ends *of* wreathen work *of* pure gold.

23 And you shalt make upon the breastplate two rings of gold, and shalt put the two rings on the two ends of the breastplate.

24 And you shalt put the two wreathen *chains* of gold in the two rings *which are* on the ends of the breastplate.

25 And *the other* two ends of the two wreathen *chains* you shalt fasten in the two ouches, and put *them* on the shoulder pieces of the ephod before it.

26 And you shalt make two rings of gold, and you shalt put them upon the two ends of the breastplate in the border thereof, which *is* in the side of the ephod inward.

27 And two *other* rings of gold you shalt make, and shalt put them on the two sides of the ephod underneath, toward the forepart thereof, over against the *other* coupling thereof, above the curious girdle of the ephod.

28 And they shall bind the breastplate by the rings thereof unto the rings of the ephod with a lace of blue, that *it* may be above the curious girdle of the ephod, and that the breastplate be not loosed from the ephod.

29 And Aaron shall bear the names of the children of Israel in the breastplate of judgment upon his heart, when he goes in unto the holy *place*, for a memorial before the LORD continually.

30   And you shalt put in the breastplate of judgment the Urim and the Thummim; and they shall be upon Aaron's heart, when he goes in before the LORD: and Aaron shall bear the judgment of the children of Israel upon his heart before the LORD continually.

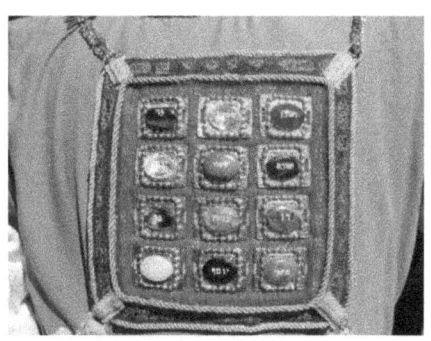

One of the most beautiful ornate pieces in the high priest's clothing is the breastplate of judgement. The great commentator Matthew Henry points out something we all need to notice. While the "breastplate of judgement is an emblem of honor," it is attached to the Ephod, which is a garment of service. The way it is attached, the two cannot be separated. He also said, "If any man will minister unto the Lord and do his will, he shall know his doctrine."

Dr. J. Vernon McGee connected the breastplate of judgement to the breastplate of righteousness. He asked why it was a breastplate of judgement and concluded that sin is judged. We need the breastplate of righteousness shown to us first in Isaiah 59:17 and later in Ephesians 6:14 if we are to stand before God. Our righteousness is not our own. It exists solely because of what Jesus has done for us through His work on the cross.

Dear Lord Jesus,

Help me see the might and power in Your Word so that I can share its glory with others. Help me that I may stand where you desire, even when alone, for you have done so much for me. Lord, forgive my unwillingness and stubbornness. Lord, help me to do that which You desire over my own wishes.

In Jesus name, Amen.

DAY #88
EXODUS 28: 31-39

31 And you shalt make the robe of the ephod all *of* blue.
32 And there shall be an hole in the top of it, in the midst thereof: it shall have a binding of woven work round about the hole of it, as it were the hole of an habergeon, that it be not rent.
33 And *beneath* upon the hem of it you shalt make pomegranates *of* blue, and *of* purple, and *of* scarlet, round about the hem thereof; and bells of gold between them round about:
34 A golden bell and a pomegranate, a golden bell and a pomegranate, upon the hem of the robe round about.
35 And it shall be upon Aaron to minister: and his sound shall be heard when he goes in unto the holy *place* before the LORD, and when he cometh out, that he die not.
36 And you shalt make a plate *of* pure gold, and grave upon it, *like* the engravings of a signet, HOLINESS TO THE LORD.
37 And you shalt put it on a blue lace, that it may be upon the mitre; upon the forefront of the mitre it shall be.

38   And it shall be upon Aaron's forehead, that Aaron may bear the iniquity of the holy things, which the children of Israel shall hallow in all their holy gifts; and it shall be always upon his forehead, that they may be accepted before the LORD.

39   And you shalt embroider the coat of fine linen, and you shalt make the mitre *of* fine linen, and you shalt make the girdle *of* needlework.

This robe is a simple piece of fabric that fits over the head. Its bells will tell where the high priest is and his movements when in the Most Holy Place.

The miter is a simple piece of headgear worn by the high priest. It does not resemble the miters seen in the Catholic church today, as pictured below. What is interesting is the lack of detail about the color of the hat. This leaves a lot to the artist's imagination. You can find blue miters, white miters, and white with blue stripes. That is not what is important to God. What is, is the gold strip with the words, "Holiness to God." Holiness is something we should work on each and every minute of the day. We are to be separate. Set apart from this world because it is not our home. Our home is in heaven,

---

Dear Lord Jesus,

Work on me. Work on me so that I may leave those things that distract me from worshipping you and putting you first. Lord, please make my life to be an example of your love so that others may see you in me.

In Jesus name, Amen.

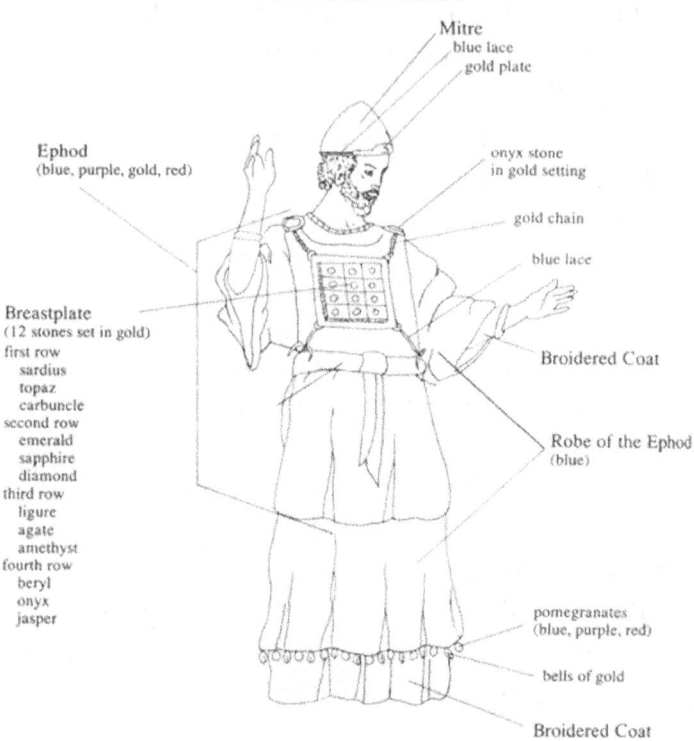

DAY #89
EXODUS 28:40-43

40 And for Aaron's sons you shalt make coats, and you shalt make for them girdles, and bonnets shalt you make for them, for glory and for beauty.

41 And you shalt put them upon Aaron your brother, and his sons with him; and shalt anoint them, and consecrate them, and sanctify them, that they may minister unto me in the priest's office.

42   And you shalt make them linen breeches to cover their nakedness; from the loins even unto the thighs they shall reach:

43   And they shall be upon Aaron, and upon his sons, when they come in unto the tabernacle of the congregation, or when they come near unto the altar to minister in the holy *place*; that they bear not iniquity, and die: *it shall be* a statute for ever unto him and his seed after him.

Aaron's sons are clothed for their ministry to the Lord. Their clothing is beautiful, glorious even, but pales in comparison to that of the High Priest. Note that these garments have two purposes.

1. "that they may minister unto me in the priest's office
2. "that they bear not iniquity (sin) and die."

This sounds like a covering for sin. A special clothing to come closer to God. Something only to wear when entering the tabernacle. Matthew Henry points out the apparent connection here to the garments that are to be worn at the wedding of God's Son in Matthew 22:12-13.

12   And he saith unto him, Friend, how came you in here not having a wedding garment? And he was speechless.

13   Then said the king to the servants, Bind him hand and foot, and take him away, and cast *him* into outer darkness; there shall be weeping and gnashing of teeth.

Think about this. These garments are like unto the Armor of God we must always wear as God's chosen in spiritual warfare found in Ephesians 6.

13 Wherefore take unto you the whole armour of God, that you may be able to withstand in the evil day, and having done all, to stand.

Aaron's sons were only to wear these garments when entering the Tabernacle. We are to wear the garments always because Jesus has broken that barrier of closeness to HIM by his sacrifice on the cross. The spiritual armor is, if anything when looked on, even more beautiful and glorious than that which Aaron's sons wore as priests. We are counted as ministers unto God. We are HIS light unto the world. We are HIS beacon. HIS light in the storm. Are you standing with Christ against the evils of this world? Is your life pointing to the ONE who saves?

Dear Lord Jesus!

May you truly be praised for your glorious work on the cross that showers Your incredible love on us. Lord, may we never shun from returning that love. May we always see Your love as the thing that must shine? Now, Lord, we beg of You, that you work on us. Make us into a beacon that shines, drawing many to you. Let us be Your tool to share Your glorious name.

In Jesus name, Amen.

DAY #90
EXODUS 29:1-9

1. And this *is* the thing that you shalt do unto them to hallow them, to minister unto me in the priest's office: Take one young bullock, and two rams without blemish,
2. And unleavened bread, and cakes unleavened tempered with oil, and wafers unleavened anointed with oil: *of* wheaten flour shalt you make them.
3. And you shalt put them into one basket, and bring them in the basket, with the bullock and the two rams.
4. And Aaron and his sons you shalt bring unto the door of the tabernacle of the congregation, and shalt wash them with water.
5. And you shalt take the garments, and put upon Aaron the coat, and the robe of the ephod, and the ephod, and the breastplate, and gird him with the curious girdle of the ephod:
6. And you shalt put the mitre upon his head, and put the holy crown upon the mitre.
7. Then shalt you take the anointing oil, and pour *it* upon his head, and anoint him.
8. And you shalt bring his sons, and put coats upon them.
9. And you shalt gird them with girdles, Aaron and his sons, and put the bonnets on them: and the priest's office shall be theirs for a perpetual statute: and you shalt consecrate Aaron and his sons.

Aaron and his sons are to be consecrated, set apart for service to God. They were chosen and did not choose this position. They put on special clothes. Aaron's head is anointed with oil. This is something special that only happens to the high priest.

Jesus is our high priest. Being God, he could only be anointed by God. This happened when the Holy Spirit descended on Him in the form of a dove, and a voice from heaven was heard saying, "This is my beloved Son in whom I am well pleased" (Matt 3:17). His next public appearance, according to Luke is to read Isaiah 61:1-2 telling He was the promised one, the Messiah to those in his home town.

There is a pattern here you will see throughout scripture on the anointing. First, a person is chosen by God. Second, they are anointed. Third, they prepare for their ministry. Fourth, they embark and do what God has set them apart to do. Ask yourself what task God has set you apart for.

Dear Lord Jesus!

YOU alone are the great provider who plans to meet my needs far before I even know I have one. Lord, help me to see my calling clearer and clearer. Lord use me. Use me to share YOUR Word so that others may know of your wondrous love.

In Jesus name, Amen.

DAY #90
EXODUS 29:10-46

10 And you shalt cause a bullock to be brought before the tabernacle of the congregation: and Aaron and his sons shall put their hands upon the head of the bullock.
11 And you shalt kill the bullock before the LORD, *by* the door of the tabernacle of the congregation.
12 And you shalt take of the blood of the bullock, and put *it* upon the horns of the altar with your finger, and pour all the blood beside the bottom of the altar.
13 And you shalt take all the fat that covers the inwards, and the caul *that is* above the liver, and the two kidneys, and the fat that *is* upon them, and burn *them* upon the altar.
14 But the flesh of the bullock, and his skin, and his dung, shalt you burn with fire without the camp: it *is* a sin offering.
15 You shalt also take one ram; and Aaron and his sons shall put their hands upon the head of the ram.
16 And you shalt slay the ram, and you shalt take his blood, and sprinkle *it* round about upon the altar.
17 And you shalt cut the ram in pieces, and wash the inwards of him, and his legs, and put *them* unto his pieces, and unto his head.
18 And you shalt burn the whole ram upon the altar: it *is* a burnt offering unto the LORD: it *is* a sweet savour, an offering made by fire unto the LORD.
19 And you shalt take the other ram; and Aaron and his sons shall put their hands upon the head of the ram.
20 Then shalt you kill the ram, and take of his blood, and put *it* upon the tip of the right ear of Aaron, and upon the tip of the right ear of his sons, and upon the thumb of their right hand, and upon the great toe of their right foot, and sprinkle the blood upon the altar round about.

21 And you shalt take of the blood that *is* upon the altar, and of the anointing oil, and sprinkle *it* upon Aaron, and upon his garments, and upon his sons, and upon the garments of his sons with him: and he shall be hallowed, and his garments, and his sons, and his sons' garments with him.

22 Also you shalt take of the ram the fat and the rump, and the fat that covers the inwards, and the caul *above* the liver, and the two kidneys, and the fat that *is* upon them, and the right shoulder; for it *is* a ram of consecration:

23 And one loaf of bread, and one cake of oiled bread, and one wafer out of the basket of the unleavened bread that *is* before the LORD:

24 And you shalt put all in the hands of Aaron, and in the hands of his sons; and shalt wave them *for* a wave offering before the LORD.

25 And you shalt receive them of their hands, and burn *them* upon the altar for a burnt offering, for a sweet savour before the LORD: it *is* an offering made by fire unto the LORD.

26 And you shalt take the breast of the ram of Aaron's consecration, and wave it *for* a wave offering before the LORD: and it shall be your part.

27 And you shalt sanctify the breast of the wave offering, and the shoulder of the heave offering, which is waved, and which is heaved up, of the ram of the consecration, *even* of *that* which *is* for Aaron, and of *that* which is for his sons:

28 And it shall be Aaron's and his sons' by a statute for ever from the children of Israel: for it *is* an heave offering: and it shall be an heave offering from the children of Israel of the sacrifice of their peace offerings, *even* their heave offering unto the LORD.

29 And the holy garments of Aaron shall be his sons' after him, to be anointed therein, and to be consecrated in them.

30. *and* that son that is priest in his stead shall put them on seven days, when he cometh into the tabernacle of the congregation to minister in the holy *place*.
31. And you shalt take the ram of the consecration, and seethe his flesh in the holy place.
32. And Aaron and his sons shall eat the flesh of the ram, and the bread that *is* in the basket, *by* the door of the tabernacle of the congregation.
33. And they shall eat those things wherewith the atonement was made, to consecrate *and* to sanctify them: but a stranger shall not eat *thereof*, because they *are* holy.
34. And if ought of the flesh of the consecrations, or of the bread, remain unto the morning, then you shalt burn the remainder with fire: it shall not be eaten, because it *is* holy.
35. And thus shalt you do unto Aaron, and to his sons, according to all *things* which I have commanded you: seven days shalt you consecrate them.
36. And you shalt offer every day a bullock *for* a sin offering for atonement: and you shalt cleanse the altar, when you hast made an atonement for it, and you shalt anoint it, to sanctify it.
37. Seven days you shalt make an atonement for the altar, and sanctify it; and it shall be an altar most holy: whatsoever touches the altar shall be holy.
38. Now this *is that* which you shalt offer upon the altar; two lambs of the first year day by day continually.
39. The one lamb you shalt offer in the morning; and the other lamb you shalt offer at even: 40 And with the one lamb a tenth deal of flour mingled with the fourth part of an hin of beaten oil; and the fourth part of an hin of wine *for* a drink offering.
41. And the other lamb you shalt offer at even, and shalt do thereto according to the meat offering of the morning, and

	according to the drink offering thereof, for a sweet savour, an offering made by fire unto the LORD.
42	*This shall be* a continual burnt offering throughout your generations *at* the door of the tabernacle of the congregation before the LORD: where I will meet you, to speak there unto you.
43	And there I will meet with the children of Israel, and *the tabernacle* shall be sanctified by my glory.
44	And I will sanctify the tabernacle of the congregation, and the altar: I will sanctify also both Aaron and his sons, to minister to me in the priest's office.
45	And I will dwell among the children of Israel, and will be their God.
46	And they shall know that I *am* the LORD their God, that brought them forth out of the land of Egypt, that I may dwell among them: I *am* the LORD their God.

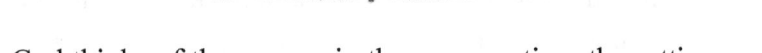

God thinks of them, even in the consecration, the setting apart of Aaron and his sons. He provides food to meet their hunger. Whichever day this starts, the consecration continues through to the seventh day. This is a holy act, after all.

Dear Lord Jesus,

Let me never forget that my home is in heaven. I am but a visitor to this earth on the way to be with You. I need to remind myself of what pleases you and what is against your will so that I may set that example of being Your desires. Lord, let me be that beacon. Let me be used by You to draw others to Your boundless love.

In Jesus name, Amen.

DAY #92
EXODUS 30:1-10

1   And you shalt make an altar to burn incense upon: *of* shittim wood shalt you make it.
2   A cubit *shall be* the length thereof, and a cubit the breadth thereof; foursquare shall it be: and two cubits *shall be* the height thereof: the horns thereof *shall be* of the same.
3   And you shalt overlay it with pure gold, the top thereof, and the sides thereof round about, and the horns thereof; and you shalt make unto it a crown of gold round about.
4   And two golden rings shalt you make to it under the crown of it, by the two corners thereof, upon the two sides of it shalt you make *it*; and they shall be for places for the staves to bear it withal.
5   And you shalt make the staves *of* shittim wood, and overlay them with gold.
6   And you shalt put it before the vail that *is* by the ark of the testimony, before the mercy seat that *is* over the testimony, where I will meet with you.
7   And Aaron shall burn thereon sweet incense every morning: when he dresses the lamps, he shall burn incense upon it.
8   And when Aaron lights the lamps at even, he shall burn incense upon it, a perpetual incense before the LORD throughout your generations.
9   You shall offer no strange incense thereon, nor burnt sacrifice, nor meat offering; neither shall you pour drink offering thereon.

10   And Aaron shall make an atonement upon the horns of it once in a year with the blood of the sin offering of atonements: once in the year shall he make atonement upon it throughout your generations: it *is* most holy unto the LORD.

The altar of incense is inside the Holy Place but by the veil, so that the incense serves not men but God.

This passage describes the altar and daily tasks Aaron, as High Priest, would be required to perform. To some, this may sound tiresome. But consider that Psalm 141:2 says, "Let my prayer be set forth before you as incense; and the lifting up of my hands as the evening sacrifice." Incense was to cover the smell of the burning flesh sacrifice, not for men but for God. Our prayers are to Jesus, who is continually before God interceding for us. Revelation 5:8 speaks of our prayers having a smell of "odors, which are the prayers of saints." We must pray always. Our prayers to God should be continually upon our lips (Ex 30:8). Ephesians 6:18 considers our prayers as part of the armor of God.

Praying always with all prayer and supplication in the Spirit, and watching thereunto with all perseverance and supplication for all saints;

Dear Lord Jesus,

May my prayers to You be continually on my lips. May my heart sing with Your wonders and praise. May worship of You, the only one true God never leaves me. May I continually pray for those who do not know You that You, upon hearing my prayers, would bang even louder to the door of their hearts that they might open that door and accept You as Lord of their life.

In Jesus name, Amen.

DAY #93
EXODUS 30:11-16

11   And the LORD spake unto Moses, saying,
12   When you take the sum of the children of Israel after their number, then shall they give every man a ransom for his soul unto the LORD, when you number them; that there be no plague among them, when *you* number them.
13   This they shall give, every one that passes among them that are numbered, half a shekel after the shekel of the sanctuary: (a shekel *is* twenty gerahs:) an half shekel *shall be* the offering of the LORD.

14   Every one that passes among them that are numbered, from twenty years old and above, shall give an offering unto the LORD.
15   The rich shall not give more, and the poor shall not give less than half a shekel, when *they* give an offering unto the LORD, to make an atonement for your souls.
16   And you shalt take the atonement money of the children of Israel, and shalt appoint it for the service of the tabernacle of the congregation; that it may be a memorial unto the children of Israel before the LORD, to make an atonement for your souls.

This required giving what some could call a tax. The census count of all who did not have a plague was first. The mention of plague is interesting because such a discovery would require that they be put outside of the camp. The age of twenty here is also mentioned. Perhaps God was telling us by this age, a person should have reached maturity.

The required atonement money was not much different for the rich or the poor. This is extremely important to understand. Souls are the same. Your soul has no less value if you are poor and no more value if you are rich. Remember, atonement is what is done to cover your sins. Psalm 22:2 says, "The rich and poor meet together: the LORD *is* the maker of them all."

Dear Lord Jesus,

You are no respecter of persons, it does not matter if a man is rich or poor; you died for all that they might have a chance to join you in glory! Lord, you do the impossible. You bring the high and mighty to the valley so they may taste your River of Water of Life which runs downhill, overflowing its banks with your grace and might. Lord may your love be known to all.

In Jesus name, Amen.

DAY #94
EXODUS 30:17

17   And the LORD spake unto Moses, saying,
18   You shalt also make a laver *of* brass, and his foot [also of] brass, to wash [withal]: and you shalt put it between the tabernacle of the congregation and the altar, and you shalt put water therein.
19   For Aaron and his sons shall wash their hands and their feet thereat:
20   When they go into the tabernacle of the congregation, they shall wash with water, that they die not; or when they come near to the altar to minister, to burn offering made by fire unto the LORD:
21   So they shall wash their hands and their feet, that they die not: and it shall be a statute for ever to them, *even* to him and to his seed throughout their generations.

The laver served to hold the water to cleanse those who served in God's Tabernacle. The picture below is an approximation of what it looked like.

Now it's important to remember the priests, Aaron's sons, already had to bathe before putting on their garments. This additional washing comes with a warning to those who did not obey this command. They would die. Having a stain of being unclean in the presence of the living God would cause death. This allows the people to think that the Tabernacle's purpose was to bring people closer to God. This washing away of uncleanness is a constant reminder of how sin separates man from God. Only God can wash away sin. You can clean your body, hands, and feet, but washing away the dirt does not take care of your heart. Psalm 24:3-5 says:

3   Who shall ascend into the hill of the LORD? or who shall stand in his holy place?
4   He that hath clean hands, **and a pure heart; who hath not lifted up his soul unto vanity, nor sworn deceitfully**.
5   He shall receive the blessing from the LORD, and righteousness from the God of his salvation.

The washing of hands and feet was important. But it is the cleanliness of the heart that matters most. A pure heart is something we cannot see. We try to see what we think is pure, but sometimes we are deceived, and a person is simply wearing a mask of a pure heart and is, in truth caught in his own vanity. Vanity places the self above others, it places an "I know it's wrong, but I am going to do it anyway," to rule the heart of a man. This vanity opens the door to sinful actions.

Only the blood of Christ washes us free from sin. Only HIS work on the cross makes us able to withstand the devil's fiery darts. Even after giving our hearts to Christ, it is our choice to continually say "NO" to sin.

Addictions cause vanity to rise up and give place to "doing it anyways." We can beat that vanity daily, even hourly by putting God before ourselves. We can not allow ourselves to be or do something that separates us from the love of God.

This washing tool in the Tabernacle, a ritual washing station after having bathed, showed us the greatness of being washed clean. Clean from the impureness and dirtiness of sin.

Are you daily calling on God and praising His name for His wondrous work on the cross?

Dear Lord Jesus,

May I seek YOUR Word daily, May I continually place YOU above my own thoughts and desires. For you daily seek what is good for me in your provision. You meet my needs before I know them. You plan long ahead to provide me with blessings. Lord, help me to do that which I should. Help me to put off all my vanity and place you on the throne of my life. Help me to never forget YOU belong there and that my life is better when I do Your will.

Lord, forgive my willing sinfulness. Wash me clean from the sins I have done and caused. Lord, I beg of You that I may be Yours forever more.

In Jesus name, Amen.

DAY #95
EXODUS 30:22-38

22 Moreover the LORD spake unto Moses, saying,
23 Take you also unto you principal spices, of pure myrrh five hundred *shekels*, and of sweet cinnamon half so much, *even* two hundred and fifty *shekels*, and of sweet calamus two hundred and fifty *shekels*,
24 And of cassia five hundred *shekels*, after the shekel of the sanctuary, and of oil olive an hin:
25 And you shalt make it an oil of holy ointment, an ointment compound after the art of the apothecary: it shall be an holy anointing oil.
26 And you shalt anoint the tabernacle of the congregation therewith, and the ark of the testimony,
27 And the table and all his vessels, and the candlestick and his vessels, and the altar of incense,
28 And the altar of burnt offering with all his vessels, and the laver and his foot.
29 And you shalt sanctify them, that they may be most holy: whatsoever touches them shall be holy.
30 And you shalt anoint Aaron and his sons, and consecrate them, that *they* may minister unto me in the priest's office.

31 And you shalt speak unto the children of Israel, saying, This shall be an holy anointing oil unto me throughout your generations.

32 Upon man's flesh shall it not be poured, neither shall you make *any other* like it, after the composition of it: it *is* holy, *and* it shall be holy unto you.

33 Whosoever compounds *any* like it, or whosoever puts *any* of it upon a stranger, shall even be cut off from his people.

34 And the LORD said unto Moses, Take unto you sweet spices, stacte, and onycha, and galbanum; *these* sweet spices with pure frankincense: of each shall there be a like *weight*:

35 And you shalt make it a perfume, a confection after the art of the apothecary, tempered together, pure *and* holy:

36 And you shalt beat *some* of it very small, and put of it before the testimony in the tabernacle of the congregation, where I will meet with you: it shall be unto you most holy.

37 And *as for* the perfume which you shalt make, you shall not make to yourselves according to the composition thereof: it shall be unto you holy for the LORD.

38 Whosoever shall make like unto that, to smell thereto, shall even be cut off from his people.

Here we have scented oil for anointing and incense that is only ever to be made for its intended purpose. Anyone who would dare to disagree and would choose to make these recipes for themselves would be committing an act of intended separation. They would be separating themselves from the God who loves them.

Oil symbolically represents the Holy Spirit. As oil is used not to anoint here and not poured out, a man does not take a bath in it, its purpose is not to enhance the physical body but to enhance remembrance of the God who saves. It separates; it brings glory not to the one who receives the anointing but to the one and only true God for whom they are anointed.

The incense represents the sweet smell of prayer to this loving God. This tells us that we may not see things the same way that God does. When we think of all the prayers, blessings, and pleadings God must ceaselessly hear from us, it is overwhelming. The closest thing we can think of is our children when small, ceaselessly asking us questions and asking for things continually, so much so that we get annoyed. So we might even think of such ceaseless prayers as annoying. BUT GOD sees our prayers as a sweet smell! Isn't that a reason to pray even more?

Dear Lord Jesus,

You are truly precious and beyond description. Your love for us is so great that you call our prayers a sweet smell. Lord, you answer our prayers. You go beyond and bless us with many things we can not comprehend. Lord, may you be glorified. May Your name be lifted up! Lord, use me so that I may show others reasons to worship you.

In Jesus name, Amen.

DAY #96
EXODUS 31:1-11

1 And the LORD spake unto Moses, saying,
2 See, I have called by name Bezaleel the son of Uri, the son of Hur, of the tribe of Judah:
3 And I have filled him with the spirit of God, in wisdom, and in understanding, and in knowledge, and in all manner of workmanship,
4 To devise cunning works, to work in gold, and in silver, and in brass,
5 And in cutting of stones, to set *them*, and in carving of timber, to work in all manner of workmanship.
6 And I, behold, I have given with him Aholiab, the son of Ahisamach, of the tribe of Dan: and in the hearts of all that are wise hearted I have put wisdom, that they may make all that I have commanded you;
7 The tabernacle of the congregation, and the ark of the testimony, and the mercy seat that *is* thereupon, and all the furniture of the tabernacle,
8 And the table and his furniture, and the pure candlestick with all his furniture, and the altar of incense,
9 And the altar of burnt offering with all his furniture, and the laver and his foot,
10 And the cloths of service, and the holy garments for Aaron the priest, and the garments of his sons, to minister in the priest's office,
11 And the anointing oil, and sweet incense for the holy *place*: according to all that I have commanded you shall they do.

In Christian circles, Bezaleel and Aholiab are only thought of when reading this chapter. They are two of God's chosen vessels to work on the Tabernacle and all that is within it. You would think these two names would be known and revered. But the God we serve places humbleness as important. We must be less so that He may be more.

God states the reason he chose Bezaleel after naming him. GOD filled Bezaleel with wisdom and understanding in all manner of workmanship. GOD did this. it was GOD who appointed Bezaleel here, not Moses. Matthew Henry points out another interesting point about Bezaleel. They left slavery in Egypt. There could not have been many who were trained craftsmen. The job given to Bezaleel by GOD is the position of Head Contractor today. This is the man who designates tasks, the man who plans and then makes sure each person has the task he/she needs to do.

Matthew Henry takes special note that Bezaleel was the grandson of Hur. He reminds us that Hur was with Moses and Aaron when they fought Amalek. Moses held the staff of God above his head. Aaron and Hur helped by supporting Moses' arms. (17:8-12). Hur was also part of the government after Aaron (24:14). His ability to get things done must have been known. It's also a Jewish tradition that Bezaleel was Miriam's husband.

But he is not to do this alone. Aholiab, of the tribe of Dan, is appointed. Aholiab is from Dan, a lesser tribe, this was actually a unifying action by God. This choice likely unified the children of Israel. Like Bezaleel, Aholiab is also chosen for his knowledge and skill: "in the hearts of all that are wise hearted I have put wisdom, that they may make all that I have commanded you."

God prepared these men for this moment for a long time. They were likely known as the best at what they do. How long had God prepared them for this moment? This God of ours is one long-range planner!

Dear Lord Jesus,

May YOU alone be praised. You work on us and mold us making us into the vessels we need to be to do your will. What we do one day may seem menial, but you work on us. Lord, help us never to forget you are molding us into something special. You are faithful to complete Your work in us. Mold us that we may be the ones You use to draw more to love you!

In Jesus name, Amen.

DAY #97
EXODUS 31:12-18

12 And the LORD spake unto Moses, saying,
13 Speak you also unto the children of Israel, saying, Verily my sabbaths you shall keep: for it *is* a sign between me and you throughout your generations; that *you* may know that I *am* the LORD that does sanctify you.
14 You shall keep the sabbath therefore; for it *is* holy unto you: every one that defiles it shall surely be put to death: for whosoever doeth *any* work therein, that soul shall be cut off from among his people.
15 Six days may work be done; but in the seventh *is* the sabbath of rest, holy to the LORD: whosoever doeth *any* work in the sabbath day, he shall surely be put to death.

16   Wherefore the children of Israel shall keep the sabbath, to observe the sabbath throughout their generations, *for* a perpetual covenant.

17   It *is* a sign between me and the children of Israel for ever: for *in* six days the LORD made heaven and earth, and on the seventh day he rested, and was refreshed.

18   And he gave unto Moses, when he had made an end of communing with him upon mount Sinai, two tables of testimony, tables of stone, written with the finger of God.

The Sabbath, the seventh day kept from all work, the day of rest, is of such importance that God stresses it over and over with Moses. Why? Because God says it is "a sign between you throughout your generations and me; that *you* may know that I *am* the LORD that does sanctify you" (vs. 13).

A sign – the sabbath separates the Jewish people from everyone else for a day of rest during this time. An entire day may have been viewed as a holiday, a rarity. But one day off every 7? It had not been done. The funny thing, in truth, is who it truly benefits. US! Once you get into a regular mode of preparing for the sabbath day and do actually recharge and relax. You become healthier. Oh, we all know a workaholic who insists that a day off is a waste of time. They can't sit still. They can't trust that the next minute can happen without them doing something unless they are sleeping. Some of them actually have problems sleeping because they do not understand the importance of rest.

Christians take their sabbath on Sundays as a celebration of the day Jesus rose from the dead. The marrying of the Jewish sabbath with the Christian Sabbath created what is called the five day work week. God seemed to know this would happen. He does not demand we work for six days and then take off a day. No, he says, "six days of work may be done." Forethought is shown here by our amazing God, who knows everything!

The sad thing is that some people decided they needed to define what work was and what it wasn't. Doing this introduced legalistic views of what could be done and what could not be done. Some orthodox Jews have even written 39 categories of work that can not be done on the sabbath. Believe it or not, this includes writing and drawing, the use of an eraser too.

Enjoy your sabbath. Take this precious important requirement of God as important for your health. Rest and recharge once every seven days.

Dear Lord Jesus,

May I not forget how important Your Word is. Lord, Your wisdom precedes the ages. We need rest. You knew this before we did! Lord help me to see rest as your prescription for living a healthier life. Lord help me to do that which is right. Let my observance of the sabbath be as You desire.

In Jesus name, Amen.

DAY #98
EXODUS 32:1-10

1   And when the people saw that Moses delayed to come down out of the mount, the people gathered themselves together unto Aaron, and said unto him, Up, make us gods,

which shall go before us; for *as for* this Moses, the man that brought us up out of the land of Egypt, we wot not what is become of him.

2 And Aaron said unto them, Break off the golden earrings, which *are* in the ears of your wives, of your sons, and of your daughters, and bring *them* unto me.

3 And all the people brake off the golden earrings which *were* in their ears, and brought *them* unto Aaron.

4 And he received *them* at their hand, and fashioned it with a graving tool, after he had made it a molten calf: and they said, These *be* your gods, O Israel, which brought you up out of the land of Egypt.

5 And when Aaron saw *it*, he built an altar before it; and Aaron made proclamation, and said, To morrow *is* a feast to the LORD.

6 And they rose up early on the morrow, and offered burnt offerings, and brought peace offerings; and the people sat down to eat and to drink, and rose up to play.

7 And the LORD said unto Moses, Go, get you down; for your people, which you broughtest out of the land of Egypt, have corrupted *themselves*:

8 They have turned aside quickly out of the way which I commanded them: they have made them a molten calf, and have worshipped it, and have sacrificed thereunto, and said, These *be* your gods, O Israel, which have brought you up out of the land of Egypt.

9 And the LORD said unto Moses, I have seen this people, and, behold, it *is* a stiffnecked people:

10 Now therefore let me alone, that my wrath may wax hot against them, and that I may consume them: and I will make of you a great nation.

Whenever this passage comes up in my reading of the Bible, I find myself pausing in wonder. This group of people had seen many amazing wonders. Not one of them could deny what God has done amongst them. Not one of the children of Israel could claim that their God had not fed them with bread from heaven. They had received the Ten Commandments. Moses had brought them to close so they could meet their God.

There are two other important lessons here also. Aaron was not God's chosen. Moses was. Moses lifted up his brother. Being God's chosen vs. claiming you have a calling is something else. The third lesson here is on leadership. Aaron was not a natural leader in many ways. He could be manipulated by the people. A leader is to be a servant of the people he leads. But he is not to be led by their desires. Just as a Godly man stands alone when others seek what is wrong. A leader should be directing the waywardness of his people back toward God. A leader has vision and hope. He directs his people in the right direction and inspires them to do what is best for them.

As simple as it gets, be like Moses, not like Aaron.

Dear Lord Jesus,

Help me to see that which is your will. Help me to not do that which is not of your will. My path needs your direction. I will seek Your Word and fill myself with its wisdom. I will eat and drink Your Word. I need to do that which is YOUR desire, not my own. Lord, guide my steps. Lord, mold me after YOUR will. Use me that I may draw others to you.

In Jesus name, Amen.

DAY #99
EXODUS 32:11-20

11 And Moses besought the LORD his God, and said, LORD, why doth your wrath wax hot against your people, which you hast brought forth out of the land of Egypt with great power, and with a mighty hand?

12 Wherefore should the Egyptians speak, and say, For mischief did he bring them out, to slay them in the mountains, and to consume them from the face of the earth? Turn from your fierce wrath, and repent of this evil against your people.

13 Remember Abraham, Isaac, and Israel, your servants, to whom you swore by your own self, and said unto them, I will multiply your seed as the stars of heaven, and all this land that I have spoken of will I give unto your seed, and they shall inherit *it* for ever.

14 And the LORD repented of the evil which he thought to do unto his people.

15 And Moses turned, and went down from the mount, and the two tables of the testimony *were* in his hand: the tables *were* written on both their sides; on the one side and on the other *were* they written.

16 And the tables *were* the work of God, and the writing *was* the writing of God, graven upon the tables.

17 And when Joshua heard the noise of the people as they shouted, he said unto Moses, *There is* a noise of war in the camp.

18   And he said, *It is* not the voice of *them that* shout for mastery, neither *is it* the voice of *them that* cry for being overcome: *but* the noise of *them that* sing do I hear.
19   And it came to pass, as soon as he came nigh unto the camp, that he saw the calf, and the dancing: and Moses' anger waxed hot, and he cast the tables out of his hands, and brake them beneath the mount.
20   And he took the calf which they had made, and burnt *it* in the fire, and ground *it* to powder, and strawed *it* upon the water, and made the children of Israel drink *of it*.

The people who God delivered from slavery have abandoned HIM and made an idol to worship. God had done many wonders in Egypt. He parted the Red Sea for their escape. He provided them with manna and birds for food when there was none. He made them triumph over trained enemy warriors. Yet, they forgot HIM! Righteous anger. The rightly deserved anger of God would have blotted them out from the earth but for Moses' intercession. Here we have established the power of prayer. The power of one man's prayer. Moses interceded before he saw the depravity of what his people were doing.

He must have felt a strong desire to descend the mountain. Joshua's words are recorded on the descent, not Moses' response. This demonstrates their lack of comprehension and understanding of what they encountered. God was so-so-right when he called these people "stiff-necked!"

Moses' own indignation rises to a level where he cannot control his actions. He throws down the very tablets that God engraved. Moses may have become even angrier realizing what he had done after that. A man horrified with what he saw racing down the mountain must have shocked the people. They had to hear him shouting and yelling at them. Joshua, the great warrior, and his aide followed him.

The people were naked— to their shame, they were celebrating being sinful, having thrown off one of the first things God gave to man. CLOTHING!

Moses has the idol broken, melted down, and ground into powder. This was not a quick thing. This did not happen in minutes. It took time. Days. When it was done, Moses poured the gold from the idol, now wasted. This was a drink of bitterness.

It's possible some thought this was all the punishment that would happen. But they had to know better. They had to feel like a child sent to his/her room after doing something so bad for the parent to acquire the needed time to cool off.

Think about the time you waited after being sent to your room for some horrible thing you had done as a child. A time that you are dreading whatever is to come. Having no knowledge that your parents may have been calling out to God for what to do. A time they may have spent pleading to God for your soul. A time they could have spent praying to God to reveal to them what they were doing wrong so that you could do the deed they had sent you to your room for.

What is not talked about here is that Moses could have been coming down the mountain with the blessings of God to share with HIS people. This could have been a time of celebration and feasting instead of a time of impending punishment. As Christians, we have to be wary that our actions are often more important than our words. We have to think about what is good and right and do what ever we can to follow God's will, not that which makes our lives easier. None of us wants to live in a state of waiting for impending punishment.

Dear Lord Jesus,

Please forgive my stupidity, my will ignorance, my sinful actions, and those things I have done not intentionally that were against your will. Lord, help me to seek Your will above my own. Lord, help me that I should put you always first, above my own selfish desires. Lord, may this be something that causes others to see YOU instead of me.

In Jesus name, Amen.

DAY #100
EXODUS 32:21-24

21   And Moses said unto Aaron, What did this people unto you, that you hast brought so great a sin upon them?
22   And Aaron said, Let not the anger of my lord wax hot: you know the people, that they *are set* on mischief.
23   For they said unto me, Make us gods, which shall go before us: for *as for* this Moses, the man that brought us up out of the land of Egypt, we wot not what is become of him.
24   And I said unto them, Whosoever hath any gold, let them break *it* off. So they gave *it* me: then I cast it into the fire, and there came out this calf.

Here we have one of the stupidest lies ever told. Most elementary-age children would know better! When Aaron was caught red-handed, he knew he was in trouble. It is possible he thought

Moses and Joshua were dead. Forty days is a long time to be alone as a leader. Forty days without hearing from Moses about what God wants had to be painful. Worse, the people were coming to him and asking for his wisdom and his wisdom came from listening to his brother. He did not have that direct connection to God like his brother. He could only have that connection if he created a god he controlled. But then, if he did that, he had to know there would be no more miracles. Yet, he would stay in control for just a little longer.

Aaron's whopper tells us one more thing. He was a terrible liar. He wasn't used to lying. He got caught and attempted to weasel his way out, and he knew that his brother would know the truth. He had never thought of what to say if Moses did return.

Aaron was trying to "dig his way out of a hole he had dug for himself." The problem here is that digging still goes deeper…not back up to the surface and out of the problem. How often do we do this today? We get caught in doing something we know is wrong and don't own up to it. Sometimes we simply hope someone else gets blamed. Doing this type of thing is not being honest at all. We have to beg God not to stop molding us into what he sees as good. We need to be HIS representatives on earth. We have to think of how people see HIM in us. What does that mean for so you?

Dear Lord Jesus,

We know there are so many stupid things we do that are wrong. Lord help us to make better choices. Help us to choose to seek that which is right. Let our words be measured and found to be carrying the weight of truth. Lord, please work on us so that we become Your light to the world.

In Jesus name, Amen.

DAY #101
EXODUS 32:25-35

25   And when Moses saw that the people *were* naked; (for Aaron had made them naked unto *their* shame among their enemies:)

26   Then Moses stood in the gate of the camp, and said, Who *is* on the LORD'S side? *let him come* unto me. And all the sons of Levi gathered themselves together unto him.

27   And he said unto them, Thus says the LORD God of Israel, Put every man his sword by his side, *and* go in and out from gate to gate throughout the camp, and slay every man his brother, and every man his companion, and every man his neighbour.

28   And the children of Levi did according to the word of Moses: and there fell of the people that day about three thousand men.

29   For Moses had said, Consecrate yourselves to day to the LORD, even every man upon his son, and upon his brother; that he may bestow upon you a blessing this day.

30   And it came to pass on the morrow, that Moses said unto the people, Ye have sinned a great sin: and now I will go up unto the LORD; peradventure I shall make an atonement for your sin.

31   And Moses returned unto the LORD, and said, Oh, this people have sinned a great sin, and have made them gods of gold.

32   Yet now, if you wilt forgive their sin--; and if not, blot me, I pray you, out of your book which you hast written.

33 And the LORD said unto Moses, Whosoever hath sinned against me, him will I blot out of my book.
34 Therefore now go, lead the people unto *the place* of which I have spoken unto you: behold, mine Angel shall go before you: nevertheless in the day when I visit I will visit their sin upon them.
35 And the LORD plagued the people, because they made the calf, which Aaron made.

Moses sees the people in their sins. Sin lays bare. It makes you naked, unclothed, and embarrassed IF you recognize the sin. Otherwise, you strut about with pride in your sin and the nakedness of your evil on display. For sin is an evil committed not against man but against God.

Moses arms those who stand with him. It seems a pitiful few who stand with him. Consider there are over a million Israelites with him. Moses sends them out to slay those who pushed this evil upon all. These would be their brothers, their relations. Some 3,000 are killed. This is a price paid for such a sin. It was man's attempt to pay the price for the sin.

When Moses goes before God, he may have wanted to say as their leader, he exacted a price for their rebellion against God. But Moses starts by openly confessing the sins of the people. Next, he begs for their forgiveness. He even offered himself if God would cut off the people. He stands with them. He intercedes for and with them. He is not separate from them. Many caught in their sins try to separate themselves from those they were sinning with, hoping it will hide the depths of their own sin.

God's answer reveals who our GOD truly is. He promises to deal with each and every person's sin. He does not abandon them. This was a possibility. It has to be thought of. Man separated himself from God. Yet, God chose still to send a messenger to them. He sent the angel, what we call a pre-incarnate image of Christ, to lead the Israelites.

God has not said he forgives their sin. But here, he acts as a loving teacher. He will not punish every one. He is willing to work with those who diligently seek him. Yet the sin of the individual will be addressed.

Oh, what an incredible miracle we have in the sacrificial love of Jesus. We have an intercessor for our sins. We have such a one whose blood covers the evil of our choices. Is this not a reason to give praise and glory to God?

Dear Lord Jesus,

Help us to make choices that separate us from doing what is easy and sinful. Help us to become your light in the darkness. Let us become beacons of YOUR love. Never let us forget how important it is to come before You and confess our sins when we do that which is wrong. Lord, You are the only one worthy of our praise. You deserve more than we can ever give You.

In Jesus name, Amen.

DAY #102
EXODUS 33:1-6

1   And the LORD said unto Moses, Depart, *and* go up hence, you and the people which you hast brought up out of the

land of Egypt, unto the land which I sware unto Abraham, to Isaac, and to Jacob, saying, Unto your seed will I give it:

2 And I will send an angel before you; and I will drive out the Canaanite, the Amorite, and the Hittite, and the Perizzite, the Hivite, and the Jebusite:

3 Unto a land flowing with milk and honey: for I will not go up in the midst of you; for you *art* a stiff-necked people: lest I consume you in the way.

4 And when the people heard these evil tidings, they mourned: and no man did put on him his ornaments.

5 For the LORD had said unto Moses, Say unto the children of Israel, Ye *are* a stiff-necked people: I will come up into the midst of you in a moment, and consume you: therefore now put off your ornaments from you, that I may know what to do unto you.

6 And the children of Israel stripped themselves of their ornaments by the mount Horeb.

When God is not happy, He removes HIS presence from where He was. The Israelites knew that their God was present with them. They had received incredible blessings. They had seen things only God could do. The impossible became a reality in front of them daily. They should have known the evil they were doing. Now God is talking about removing His presence from them.

Yet God says he will keep his promise. Despite all that they had done, God did not break his promise. They were to be given that promised land. They had heard this promise so many times as slaves in the land of Egypt. They had never forgotten the promise. That promise was repeated from fathers and mothers to their children. They knew this promise. Better yet, this generation knew they were the ones that were to receive that blessing… BUT they ruined their blessing by separating themselves from God. The next generation would see it.

The people mourned the penalty for their sins. They may not have grasped until that moment what that penalty would be. There had to be a pervading sense of dread in the camp. They had spit in the face of God. Would he annihilate them?

This God asked only for them to put off their ornaments. Things like jewelry, accessories, and more. Things that made them seem or feel special. They were not special now.

How would you have felt waiting …? Would you have been shaking, fearing whatever was to happen?

Dear Lord Jesus,

You are the perfect and great GOD. The only one worthy of our worship. You came to us when we were yet in our sin. You paid the price for the judgement we so deserve for our sins. Lord use me. Allow me to be used to be Your light in the world. Guide me that I may be the one who shines a beacon directly to Your love for the lost.

In Jesus name, Amen.

DAY #103
EXODUS 33:7-23

7   And Moses took the tabernacle, and pitched it without the camp, afar off from the camp, and called it the Tabernacle

of the congregation. And it came to pass, *that* every one which sought the LORD went out unto the tabernacle of the congregation, which *was* without the camp.

8 And it came to pass, when Moses went out unto the tabernacle, *that* all the people rose up, and stood every man *at* his tent door, and looked after Moses, until he was gone into the tabernacle.

9 And it came to pass, as Moses entered into the tabernacle, the cloudy pillar descended, and stood *at* the door of the tabernacle, and *the LORD* talked with Moses.

10 And all the people saw the cloudy pillar stand *at* the tabernacle door: and all the people rose up and worshipped, every man *in* his tent door.

11 And the LORD spake unto Moses face to face, as a man speaketh unto his friend. And he turned again into the camp: but his servant Joshua, the son of Nun, a young man, departed not out of the tabernacle.

12 And Moses said unto the LORD, See, you sayest unto me, Bring up this people: and you hast not let me know whom you wilt send with me. Yet you hast said, I know you by name, and you hast also found grace in my sight.

13 Now therefore, I pray you, if I have found grace in your sight, shew me now your way, that I may know you, that I may find grace in your sight: and consider that this nation *is* your people.

14 And he said, My presence shall go *with you*, and I will give you rest.

15 And he said unto him, If your presence go not *with me*, carry us not up hence.

16 For wherein shall it be known here that I and people have found grace in your sight? *is it* not in that you go with us? so shall we be separated, I and your people, from all the people that *are* upon the face of the earth.

17	And the LORD said unto Moses, I will do this thing also that you hast spoken: for you hast found grace in my sight, and I know you by name.
18	And he said, I beseech you, shew me your glory.
19	And he said, I will make all my goodness pass before you, and I will proclaim the name of the LORD before you; and will be gracious to whom I will be gracious, and will shew mercy on whom I will shew mercy.
20	And he said, You canst not see my face: for there shall no man see me, and live.
21	And the LORD said, Behold, *there is* a place by me, and you shalt stand upon a rock:
22	And it shall come to pass, while my glory passeth by, that I will put you in a clift of the rock, and will cover you with my hand while I pass by:
23	And I will take away mine hand, and you shalt see my back parts: but my face shall not be seen.

The tabernacle here was not the one that God had instructed Moses to build. It was a separate tent that Moses had used to meet with God. Can you imagine how you would feel if your pastor had the ability to suddenly yank your church up and transfer it miles away? No warning. How would you react? Especially if you were part of a group that had publicly embarrassed him to have been your pastor.

I can only imagine the shock and awe of watching Moses and Joshua take down the tent. Then the compulsion to do exactly what the Israelites did, watched, and followed. A deep sadness was forming in your heart as never before. I would have felt like crying out. Is there nothing that we can do to be forgiven?

Moses still understood the incredible penalty they faced. His people did not grasp what they had done. Can you imagine them watching and seeing the awesome power of God descending as a pillar of cloud before Moses?

Moses had said to them to put off their ornaments, for God was coming into their midst. When they saw that cloud, the presence of God, they had to feel the weight of their sin as even greater than they ever imagined.

God says to Moses things that change everything in this short conversation.

1) "My presence shall go with you, and I will give you rest."
2) "You have found grace in my sight; I know by your name."
3) "I will make my goodness pass before you…I will proclaim the name of the Lord before you."
4) "I will show mercy on whom I will show mercy."

God here shows himself so much bigger and greater than we can grasp. He shows himself to be personal. He looks at us as individuals, not as a group. He may judge the group, but each person is responsible for how he/she responds to God.

God here promises one more thing. One thing that the Israelites needed above all. He promised to go before them. It is how HE goes before them that must be paid attention to. HIS goodness passes before them. In other words, HIS blessings will be present when they approach a group of people because GOD is present. Even bigger yet, God does not need Moses to say who God is. God is real. He is not some imaginary thing that needs a man to speak on His behalf. God chose Moses, but he did not need him.

One more thing that must be discussed is: If you were present seeing all of this as Joshua did, how would you react? Joshua was basically an aide, a servant. The man who did whatever he was asked by Moses. He did not have a leadership position that we know of at this time. What value did a warrior have when God fights for you? Can you imagine being a person who thought himself strong suddenly in the presence of the living God? I know I would have had questions of my own for God. Joshua had a chance to be in God's presence alone here! What would you have said or done in his place?

Dear Lord Jesus,

You alone are worthy of our worship. You do go ahead of us. You do bring the goodness and mercy that precedes us. Lord God, I ask that you make us into a people whose words and actions proclaim YOUR love to all. May it be impossible for those who do not have a relationship with You to see that they know of someone who has a relationship with YOU! Our lives stood out as a way to live and commune with the great I AM. Lord, let us also share who you are with those we are yet to know. Let us be bold, for YOU are present!

In Jesus name, Amen.

DAY #104
EXODUS 34:1-4

1   And the LORD said unto Moses, Hew thee two tables of stone like unto the first: and I will write upon *these* tables the words that were in the first tables, which you brakest.

2   And be ready in the morning, and come up in the morning unto mount Sinai, and present yourself there to me in the top of the mount.

3   And no man shall come up with you, neither let any man be seen throughout all the mount; neither let the flocks nor herds feed before that mount.

4   And he hewed two tables of stone like unto the first; and Moses rose up early in the morning, and went up unto mount Sinai, as the LORD had commanded him, and took in his hand the two tables of stone.

There is a lot in this small passage that must be looked at. The Lord first gave Moses the law by writing it down and cutting the stone tablets out for Moses to carry. Moses, in the midst of righteous anger when his people chose to make and serve another god, had destroyed the tablets that were the work of God. Now Moses has to cut the stone tablets and ready them. This is not a brief process. It takes time. Note here that God says HE will write upon these tablets. God uses man to get HIS Word to the people. In the sixty-six books of the Bible, God used men as vessels to communicate HIS Word.

When God communicates with those of a repentant heart, He writes the law in their hearts. Individuals need to recognize their sinful nature for this to happen. Hebrews 8:10 says: "For this *is* the covenant that I will make with the house of Israel after those days, saith the Lord; I will put my laws into their mind, and write them in their hearts: and I will be to them a God, and they shall be to me a people." God deals with what is inside of us. He desires what motivates and drives us should be a heart after Him. For this reason, He works on hearts writing his law. Cutting out that which is not of Him giving place for our love of the LOVING GOD to grow.

Deuteronomy 30:6 "And the LORD your God will circumcise thine heart, and the heart of your seed, to love the LORD your God with all thine heart, and with all your soul, that you mayest live."

Jeremiah 31:33 "But this *shall be* the covenant that I will make with the house of Israel; After those days, saith the LORD, I will put my law in their inward parts, and write it in their hearts; and will be their God, and they shall be my people."

Dear Lord Jesus,

Work on me. Work on my heart. Change me so that I may put YOU first always. May my love of You direct others to find Your loving kindness. For I am but nothing, but YOU are all and more than I can comprehend. Lord, I beg of you. Change the hearts of those I know to one that loves You. Call them to live in Your love.

In Jesus name, Amen.

DAY #105
EXODUS 34:5-9

5   And the LORD descended in the cloud, and stood with him there, and proclaimed the name of the LORD.
6   And the LORD passed by before him, and proclaimed, The LORD, The LORD God, merciful and gracious, longsuffering, and abundant in goodness and truth,
7   Keeping mercy for thousands, forgiving iniquity and transgression and sin, and that will by no means clear *the guilty*;

	visiting the iniquity of the fathers upon the children, and upon the children's children, unto the third and to the fourth *generation.*
8	And Moses made haste, and bowed his head toward the earth, and worshipped.
9	And he said, If now I have found grace in your sight, O Lord, let my Lord, I pray you, go among us; for it *is* a stiffnecked people; and pardon our iniquity and our sin, and take us for thine inheritance.

God's visits with Moses are usually private. He does not need to put on a show. But this time, God descends in the form of a cloud so the people can see God is meeting with Moses.

Verse 6 here proclaims persons in the Godhead. God shows he is one, but there is unity in his oneness.

Can you imagine leading a sinful people? And God starts to talk about his forgiving sins? Would you not be on your knees hoping and begging that this loving God would forgive their stupid sinfulness? Moses not only fell on his knees and worshiped, he asked God for forgiveness for his people.

Moses gets more of a response as a leader of a repentant people than he expects. God had said he would honor his promises to Abraham and Isaac and added a HUGE bonus. He promises to do marvels, such that no one has seen things like this before. How would you react to being told this?

Dear Lord Jesus,

You are the keeper of promises. You are the merciful and loving God. You promise great things and deliver bigger and better every time. Lord, help me to love as You love, with graciousness and forgiveness.

In Jesus name, Amen.

DAY #106
EXODUS 34:10-28

10   And he said, Behold, I make a covenant: before all your people I will do marvels, such as have not been done in all the earth, nor in any nation: and all the people among which you *are* shall see the work of the LORD: for it *is* a terrible thing that I will do with you.
11   Observe you that which I command you this day: behold, I drive out before you the Amorite, and the Canaanite, and the Hittite, and the Perizzite, and the Hivite, and the Jebusite.
12   Take heed to yourself, lest you make a covenant with the inhabitants of the land whither you go, lest it be for a snare in the midst of you:
13   But you shall destroy their altars, break their images, and cut down their groves:
14   For you shalt worship no other god: for the LORD, whose name *is* Jealous, *is* a jealous God:
15   Lest you make a covenant with the inhabitants of the land, and they go a whoring after their gods, and do sacrifice unto their gods, and *one* call you, and you eat of his sacrifice;
16   And you take of their daughters unto your sons, and their daughters go a whoring after their gods, and make your sons go a whoring after their gods.

17 You shalt make to yourself no molten gods.
18 The feast of unleavened bread shalt you keep. Seven days you shall eat unleavened bread, as I commanded you, in the time of the month Abib: for in the month Abib you came out from Egypt.
19 All that opens the matrix *is* mine; and every firstling
20 But the firstling of an ass you shalt redeem with a lamb: and if you redeem *him* not, then shalt you break his neck. All the firstborn of your sons you shalt redeem. And none shall appear before me empty.
21 Six days you shalt work, but on the seventh day you shalt rest: in earing time and in harvest you shalt rest.
22 And you shalt observe the feast of weeks, of the firstfruits of wheat harvest, and the feast of ingathering at the year's end.
23 Thrice in the year shall all your men children appear before the Lord GOD, the God of Israel.
24 For I will cast out the nations before you, and enlarge your borders: neither shall any man desire your land, when you shalt go up to appear before the LORD your God thrice in the year.
25 You shalt not offer the blood of my sacrifice with leaven; neither shall the sacrifice of the feast of the passover be left unto the morning.
26 The first of the firstfruits of your land you shalt bring unto the house of the LORD your God. You shalt not seethe a kid in his mother's milk.
27 And the LORD said unto Moses, Write you these words: for after the tenor of these words I have made a covenant with you and with Israel.
28 And he was there with the LORD forty days and forty nights; he did neither eat bread, nor drink water. And he

wrote upon the tables the words of the covenant, the ten commandments.

When you're in charge, and an underling comes to you confessing something so repugnant and horrifying, you contemplate separating them from your company. What do you do? Believe it or not, there are actually established ways to deal with issues like this. The restoration process generally includes very clear directions that require defining each direction and step so that they can be clearly judged. Look at what God has asked so far. Not one of these things is hard. Not one requires more than simple acceptance and willingness to listen and do what he asks.

There are warnings here that are prophetic of events to come. What is being asked here is nothing more than what was asked before. This is a clear re-establishment of a relationship. The element of movement was there before, but this time the concept of encountering others is introduced. Before, all that could be thought of was escape. Now there is the introduction to encountering others. Basically, God asks them not to change who they are for others.

He speaks of war, where HE leads them. He speaks of foolishness that could allow bad influence to destroy them from within. None of these things are hard. Not one. There are hints that they must guard against deception. But no clear statement that they should not trust others.

Dear Lord Jesus,

You desire our love and devotion. We are not even asked to do hard or difficult tasks to serve You. Believe…That is all You truly ask. For some, that may be hard when they are not allowed to believe in another god where they live. God, You know where we are. You know us inside and out. While there is nothing too difficult for You, you gave us the simplest of directions. You create a world where we can grow and blossom. Lord, use us. Use us that our Love of YOU may be an example of how great YOUR love is.

In Jesus name, Amen.

DAY #107
EXODUS 34:29-35

29   And it came to pass, when Moses came down from mount Sinai with the two tables of testimony in Moses' hand, when he came down from the mount, that Moses wist not that the skin of his face shone while he talked with him.

30   And when Aaron and all the children of Israel saw Moses, behold, the skin of his face shone; and they were afraid to come nigh him.

31   And Moses called unto them; and Aaron and all the rulers of the congregation returned unto him: and Moses talked with them.

32   And afterward all the children of Israel came nigh: and he gave them in commandment all that the LORD had spoken with him in mount Sinai.

33   And *till* Moses had done speaking with them, he put a vail on his face.

34   But when Moses went in before the LORD to speak with him, he took the vail off, until he came out. And he came out, and spake unto the children of Israel *that* which he was commanded.

35   And the children of Israel saw the face of Moses, that the skin of Moses' face shone: and Moses put the vail upon his face again, until he went in to speak with him.

Forty days and nights uninterrupted and alone with God was not something Moses had not done before. The first time the people rebelled against God. Moses was doing something new this time. He was fasting. Fasting means we put off the joy of eating. It's done in Christianity to draw yourself closer to God, to prepare for spiritual warfare, and to plead a cause before God. Moses was unknowingly fasting for all three reasons. He was in the presence of God for these forty days and nights. Last time he had brought Joshua to attend to his needs. This time he was alone. God took care of him. When Moses came down from the mountain, he had a glow to his skin.

Today we would not have feared so much as been inquisitive as to what caused it. We would have asked a ton of questions. Not one being, "have you been in the presence of God?"

Moses wore a veil not because he was different but because it created fear. He wanted to be able to interact with those he loved. These people whom he interceded with. He was not required to do it. It was done out of his love for his people. But with God, there was no need for such a thing. His GOD was so much bigger; he removed his veil when serving and talking with God.

Dear Lord Jesus,

You are far bigger than any fear we have. Your love for us sees us as we are. You know us inside and out. Work on us Lord, Cause us to seek YOU first. Lord, use me! Use me to lead others to YOU. Your love is so great, let me be one to share that love with others.

In Jesus name, Amen.

DAY #108
EXODUS 35:1-19

1 And Moses gathered all the congregation of the children of Israel together, and said unto them, These *are* the words which the LORD hath commanded, that *you* should do them.
2 Six days shall work be done, but on the seventh day there shall be to you an holy day, a sabbath of rest to the LORD: whosoever doeth work therein shall be put to death.
3 Ye shall kindle no fire throughout your habitations upon the sabbath day.
4 And Moses spake unto all the congregation of the children of Israel, saying, This *is* the thing which the LORD commanded, saying,
5 Take ye from among you an offering unto the LORD: whosoever *is* of a willing heart, let him bring it, an offering of the LORD; gold, and silver, and brass,
6 And blue, and purple, and scarlet, and fine linen, and goats' *hair*,
7 And rams' skins dyed red, and badgers' skins, and shittim wood,
8 And oil for the light, and spices for anointing oil, and for the sweet incense,

9   And onyx stones, and stones to be set for the ephod, and for the breastplate.
10 And every wise hearted among you shall come, and make all that the LORD hath commanded;
11 The tabernacle, his tent, and his covering, his taches, and his boards, his bars, his pillars, and his sockets,
12 The ark, and the staves thereof, *with* the mercy seat, and the vail of the covering,
13 The table, and his staves, and all his vessels, and the shewbread,
14 The candlestick also for the light, and his furniture, and his lamps, with the oil for the light,
15 And the incense altar, and his staves, and the anointing oil, and the sweet incense, and the hanging for the door at the entering in of the tabernacle,
16 The altar of burnt offering, with his brasen grate, his staves, and all his vessels, the laver and his foot,
17 The hangings of the court, his pillars, and their sockets, and the hanging for the door of the court,
18 The pins of the tabernacle, and the pins of the court, and their cords,
19 The cloths of service, to do service in the holy *place*, the holy garments for Aaron the priest, and the garments of his sons, to minister in the priest's office.

Moses delivers God's Word to the people. He begins by giving God's call to keep the sabbath day holy and set apart for HIM. Those who will not obey this simple command will be cut off from them. This means their execution.

Next, he delivers God's request for materials needed to build the Tabernacle after God's design. It may seem to some that God is asking Israel for its riches. He also asked for skilled labor. Some were jobs women were known for doing. There seemed to be enough need for materials and enough work to be done that many could have a task assigned to them. All they needed was to be told what to do.

Ever feel like you are waiting for direction and need to be told what to do?

Dear Lord Jesus!

Thank you for all You do in my life. Sometimes I just need direction. Lord, guide my feet. Point me in the right direction. Tell me where you want me and what you want me to do. Use me, God, that I may be one of those chosen vessels to share Your love.

In Jesus name, Amen.

DAY #109
EXODUS 35:20-29

20   And all the congregation of the children of Israel departed from the presence of Moses.
21   And they came, every one whose heart stirred him up, and every one whom his spirit made willing, *and* they brought the LORD'S offering to the work of the tabernacle of the congregation, and for all his service, and for the holy garments.

22　　And they came, both men and women, as many as were willing hearted, *and* brought bracelets, and earrings, and rings, and tablets, all jewels of gold: and every man that offered *offered* an offering of gold unto the LORD.

23　　And every man, with whom was found blue, and purple, and scarlet, and fine linen, and goats' *hair*, and red skins of rams, and badgers' skins, brought *them*.

24　　Every one that did offer an offering of silver and brass brought the LORD'S offering: and every man, with whom was found shittim wood for any work of the service, brought *it*.

25　　And all the women that were wise hearted did spin with their hands, and brought that which they had spun, *both* of blue, and of purple, *and* of scarlet, and of fine linen.

26　　And all the women whose heart stirred them up in wisdom spun goats' *hair*.

27　　And the rulers brought onyx stones, and stones to be set, for the ephod, and for the breastplate;

28　　And spice, and oil for the light, and for the anointing oil, and for the sweet incense.

29　　The children of Israel brought a willing offering unto the LORD, every man and woman, whose heart made them willing to bring for all manner of work, which the LORD had commanded to be made by the hand of Moses.

A repentant heart is often one that is more generous. The people of Israel willingly give up their hearts. They willingly gave the things that were required to build the temple. There was no invasion of privacy. No demands that a person gives this or that. No forced labor to create things. This was all done with a willing heart.

They did not delay in their giving. They went to where they had stored the needed items in their tents and eagerly, cheerfully gave these things to be used in the creation of the Tabernacle.

The amount of Gold, furs, royal-colored linens, and more remind us that the people of Egypt readily gave to the Hebrew people as they left. They left with the riches of Egypt. They carried these riches on their back and in their carts as they raced through the parted Red Sea. They carried these luxuries with them, not knowing that the gifts of these things were part of God's plan for this moment.

This, for some, must have been an eye-opening moment. They thought about their slave masters giving them great treasures. They were "paid" for their slavery in this respect. Yet, these luxuries would serve no purpose for them. They were on the run. Who would they exchange goods with? This was part of God's plan. It was done so that they could give to the Lord.

Perhaps that is something we do not reflect enough on. How we get paid is from God. It's part of his plan so that we may have something to offer Him.

Dear Lord Jesus,

You alone are worthy of our worship. You provide for us long before we know we have a need. You plan to meet our needs before we have a clue of that need. You even gift us with a way to give to you. Lord, may I never forget how YOU provide for me. Lord, use me to share Your great love for us.

In Jesus name, Amen.

DAY #110
EXODUS 35:30-35

30 And Moses said unto the children of Israel, See, the LORD hath called by name Bezaleel the son of Uri, the son of Hur, of the tribe of Judah;
31 And he hath filled him with the spirit of God, in wisdom, in understanding, and in knowledge, and in all manner of workmanship;
32 And to devise curious works, to work in gold, and in silver, and in brass,
33 And in the cutting of stones, to set *them*, and in carving of wood, to make any manner of cunning work.
34 And he hath put in his heart that he may teach, *both* he, and Aholiab, the son of Ahisamach, of the tribe of Dan.
35 Them hath he filled with wisdom of heart, to work all manner of work, of the engraver, and of the cunning workman, and of the embroiderer, in blue, and in purple, in scarlet, and in fine linen, and of the weaver, *even* of them that do any work, and of those that devise cunning work.

God appointed Bezaleel and Ahoilab to do the work. They were both in every sense of the phrase "one in a million." The scripture tells us they had not only a skill but also talent! But their talent and skill did not seem sufficient to them. They had the desire to know more and more. As a result, they broadened their knowledge and skills. On top of this, they had developed what we call today project management skills. If these two had lived in more recent times, they might have been called Renaissance men.

Can you imagine being Moses and being told all the details of how something is made? An architect could be comfortable hearing this. He could put it on the drawing board. But could he do the work? In today's world, that answer is generally no. God picked these two men out. Their names are forever emblazoned into history as the men who led the building of the Tabernacle and the Ark of the Covenant.

Where are your talents and skills? What can you do to improve them? Are you building on them? Are you broadening your knowledge?

Dear Lord Jesus,

May Your wisdom forever be that which I seek. Lord, may I become one to put YOU first and, in doing, seek to improve the talents and skills, You have blessed me with. Lord, help me to be one who does his best at work and home. Help me, Lord, to become one who lives a life as an example of YOUR love for us.

In Jesus name, Amen.

DAY #111
EXODUS 36:1-7

1   Then wrought Bezaleel and Aholiab, and every wise hearted man, in whom the LORD put wisdom and understanding to

	know how to work all manner of work for the service of the sanctuary, according to all that the LORD had commanded.
2	And Moses called Bezaleel and Aholiab, and every wise hearted man, in whose heart the LORD had put wisdom, *even* every one whose heart stirred him up to come unto the work to do it:
3	And they received of Moses all the offering, which the children of Israel had brought for the work of the service of the sanctuary, to make it *withal*. And they brought yet unto him free offerings every morning.
4	And all the wise men, that wrought all the work of the sanctuary, came every man from his work which they made;
5	And they spake unto Moses, saying, The people bring much more than enough for the service of the work, which the LORD commanded to make.
6	And Moses gave commandment, and they caused it to be proclaimed throughout the camp, saying, Let neither man nor woman make any more work for the offering of the sanctuary. So the people were restrained from bringing.
7	For the stuff they had was sufficient for all the work to make it, and too much.

Here we have the only recorded example in the Bible of a people giving so much that they have to be restrained. These people had been freed from slavery, and they gave freely of their own desires. They gave daily. All they knew was that what they were giving was to be used in making a Tabernacle for God. Many could not work in the building of it and wanted to do their part, so they gave, and they gave. They knew only that this work was something the God who freed them wanted. This opportunity to give was a chance to say thank you to the God who freed them. They gave enthusiastically! They gave easily. It did not hurt them. When you give to God, do you give from the heart? Do you give willingly?

Dear Lord Jesus,

You are the One who frees slaves from bondage. You are the only One worthy of worship. May my giving be blessed by You. May my giving bless Your work. Lord, use my small donations so that Your work may be done. Lord, may Your love be shared broader and with more lost souls because of what I give.

In Jesus name, Amen.

DAY #112
EXODUS 36:8-38

8   And every wise hearted man among them that wrought the work of the tabernacle made ten curtains *of* fine twined linen, and blue, and purple, and scarlet: *with* cherubims of cunning work made he them.
9   The length of one curtain *was* twenty and eight cubits, and the breadth of one curtain four cubits: the curtains *were* all of one size.
10 And he coupled the five curtains one unto another: and *the other* five curtains he coupled one unto another.
11 And he made loops of blue on the edge of one curtain from the selvedge in the coupling: likewise he made in the uttermost side of *another* curtain, in the coupling of the second.

12 Fifty loops made he in one curtain, and fifty loops made he in the edge of the curtain which *was* in the coupling of the second: the loops held one *curtain* to another.

13 And he made fifty taches of gold, and coupled the curtains one unto another with the taches: so it became one tabernacle.

14 And he made curtains *of* goats' *hair* for the tent over the tabernacle: eleven curtains he made them.

15 The length of one curtain *was* thirty cubits, and four cubits *was* the breadth of one curtain: the eleven curtains *were* of one size.

16 And he coupled five curtains by themselves, and six curtains by themselves.

17 And he made fifty loops upon the uttermost edge of the curtain in the coupling, and fifty loops made he upon the edge of the curtain which couples the second.

18 And he made fifty taches *of* brass to couple the tent together, that it might be one.

19 And he made a covering for the tent *of* rams' skins dyed red, and a covering *of* badgers' skins above *that*.

20 And he made boards for the tabernacle *of* shittim wood, standing up.

21 The length of a board *was* ten cubits, and the breadth of a board one cubit and a half.

22 One board had two tenons, equally distant one from another: thus did he make for all the boards of the tabernacle.

23 And he made boards for the tabernacle; twenty boards for the south side southward:

24 And forty sockets of silver he made under the twenty boards; two sockets under one board for his two tenons, and two sockets under another board for his two tenons.

25 And for the other side of the tabernacle, *which is* toward the north corner, he made twenty boards,

26 And their forty sockets of silver; two sockets under one board, and two sockets under another board.
27 And for the sides of the tabernacle westward he made six boards.
28 And two boards made he for the corners of the tabernacle in the two sides.
29 And they were coupled beneath, and coupled together at the head thereof, to one ring: thus he did to both of them in both the corners.
30 And there were eight boards; and their sockets *were* sixteen sockets of silver, under every board two sockets.
31 And he made bars of shittim wood; five for the boards of the one side of the tabernacle,
32 And five bars for the boards of the other side of the tabernacle, and five bars for the boards of the tabernacle for the sides westward.
33 And he made the middle bar to shoot through the boards from the one end to the other.
34 And he overlaid the boards with gold, and made their rings *of* gold *to be* places for the bars, and overlaid the bars with gold.
35 And he made a vail *of* blue, and purple, and scarlet, and fine twined linen: *with* cherubims made he it of cunning work.
36 And he made thereunto four pillars *of* shittim *wood*, and overlaid them with gold: their hooks *were of* gold; and he cast for them four sockets of silver.
37 And he made an hanging for the tabernacle door *of* blue, and purple, and scarlet, and fine twined linen, of needlework;
38 And the five pillars of it with their hooks: and he overlaid their chapiters and their fillets with gold: but their five sockets *were of* brass.

There are a few curious things to note here. First, the outside is created before the things that go within. The way this report also is a summarizing of completed projects that likely were worked on at the same time. The two men appointed to the task were talented, knew what they needed down, and could clearly designate and motivate since God appointed them. Project management is a skill that allows one person to oversee and manage many tasks at the same time. They may not even seem to go together. Think of it like this, one man comes to you and asks you to make 100 carburetors specially designed. He gives you a detailed design of what he needs. He moves on and talks to a hundred or so others. By the end of the month, he has 100 cars ready to be assembled.

There is no stated timeline to determine how long after the project was handed off to God's appointees, these were accomplished. I expected the completion to be much faster than anyone expected.

Every worker, no matter how small or seemingly insignificant, knew they had a hand in making something for God. The bosses encouraged doing your best to deliver the best quality to this God who loved them.

Your work, your job, and your chores should be considered by God. Are you giving your best?

Dear Lord Jesus,

Please remind me work is an example of YOU. I need to do my best so that YOU may be glorified. Even in tasks I do not like, Lord, cause me to be an example. Remind me that I am always standing up as an example of YOUR boundless love. Help me to be an example of YOU. Let my work be an example of how much YOU LOVE ME! Sometimes I forget this Lord. Please forgive me for that. Lord, please work on me so that I may be that one who changes things for you. Lord change my attitude towards work. Please dear God may I see it as a chance to worship and glorify You.

In Jesus name, Amen.

DAY #113
EXODUS 37:1-9

1   And Bezaleel made the ark *of* shittim wood: two cubits and a half *was* the length of it, and a cubit and a half the breadth of it, and a cubit and a half the height of it:
2   And he overlaid it with pure gold within and without, and made a crown of gold to it round about.
3   And he cast for it four rings of gold, [to be set] by the four corners of it; even two rings upon the one side of it, and two rings upon the other side of it.
4   And he made staves *of* shittim wood, and overlaid them with gold.
5   And he put the staves into the rings by the sides of the ark, to bear the ark.
6   And he made the mercy seat *of* pure gold: two cubits and a half *was* the length thereof, and one cubit and a half the breadth thereof.
7   And he made two cherubims *of* gold, beaten out of one piece made he them, on the two ends of the mercy seat;
8   One cherub on the end on this side, and another cherub on the *other* end on that side: out of the mercy seat made he the cherubims on the two ends thereof.
9   And the cherubims spread out *their* wings on high, *and* covered with their wings over the mercy seat, with their

faces one to another; *even* to the mercy seatward were the faces of the cherubims.

Can you imagine being known for the quality of your work so much that God himself makes an order of your work? This is after all that happened to Bezaleel. Would you be even more particular knowing it was for the living God? YES!

But this is not the question some are asking. They are asking why this is now so repetitive. Moses was told how things should be built. He was given great detail. The great commentator Matthew Henry said that this is because the things that were made for within the Tabernacle were not to be seen by all. Only those serving in the Tabernacle would see them. But the people needed to know these things. They needed it engraved in their hearts. The "Rule of Threes," known by many speakers, is here also. When something is important in a speech you are giving, and you want the people to remember it, you must repeat it at least three times. The work the people, were doing was known to all. But never being able to see something unless you are the High Priest – does that make it any less important to know about? The ark of the covenant could only be seen by the High Priest. Only those Levites who worked in the Tabernacle could see the other items. The people needed to know what was in there. Nothing had to be secret! Not one thing. In fact, the opposite is true. Nothing could be hidden! The people needed to be aware of all that was done. They needed to know and understand no waste had occurred. No one had stolen from the offerings. It was used as they said it would be.

Dear Lord Jesus!

Thank you for setting the example of good government and transparency. We need to learn from these examples and make them part of who we are as a people. Lord, help us to see how much Your sacrifice changed things. Lord, Your blood removed ritual offerings for our sinfulness. Your sacrifice covers us like a blanket. Once offered, covering all of our sins. This is why YOU alone are worthy of our praise! Thank you, Lord. Thank YOU for everything. Mold me that I may be an example of Your love.

In Jesus name, Amen.

DAY #114
EXODUS 37:10-24

10   And he made the table *of* shittim wood: two cubits *was* the length thereof, and a cubit the breadth thereof, and a cubit and a half the height thereof:

11   And he overlaid it with pure gold, and made thereunto a crown of gold round about.

12   Also he made thereunto a border of an handbreadth round about; and made a crown of gold for the border thereof round about.

13   And he cast for it four rings of gold, and put the rings upon the four corners that *were* in the four feet thereof.

14   Over against the border were the rings, the places for the staves to bear the table.

15   And he made the staves *of* shittim wood, and overlaid them with gold, to bear the table.

16   And he made the vessels which *were* upon the table, his dishes, and his spoons, and his bowls, and his covers to cover withal, *of* pure gold.

17   And he made the candlestick *of* pure gold: *of* beaten work made he the candlestick; his shaft, and his branch, his bowls, his knops, and his flowers, were of the same:

18   And six branches going out of the sides thereof; three branches of the candlestick out of the one side thereof, and three branches of the candlestick out of the other side thereof:

19   Three bowls made after the fashion of almonds in one branch, a knop and a flower; and three bowls made like almonds in another branch, a knop and a flower: so throughout the six branches going out of the candlestick.

20   And in the candlestick *were* four bowls made like almonds, his knops, and his flowers:

21   And a knop under two branches of the same, and a knop under two branches of the same, and a knop under two branches of the same, according to the six branches going out of it.

22   Their knops and their branches were of the same: all of it *was* one beaten work *of* pure gold.

23   And he made his seven lamps, and his snuffers, and his snuff dishes, *of* pure gold.

24   *of* a talent of pure gold made he it, and all the vessels thereof.

The table was a place that the showbread was seen. The Showbread was not there to be consumed/eaten. Jesus offers every believer a place at HIS table. We take part in a remembrance ritual of Christ, often called communion. In this, we take part in eating bread, which "represents Christ's body which was broken for you." What the law showed only a glimpse of to some, Christ offers to everyone who is willing to give of themselves to HIM.

Matthew Henry reminds us that the golden candlesticks here represent the light of "divine revelation with which God's church upon earth has always been enlightened…The Bible is a golden candlestick of pure gold, Ps. 19:10. From it light is diffused to every part of God's tabernacle…." As believers, we receive the Bible as HIS Word. Learning more about the Bible enables us to minister unto Him and to those lost in the world. Enabling us to be a light to the world.

Dear Lord Jesus,

Your Word is a light at my feet. Your Word fills me and makes me a part of Your great love, which is so great that I can't contain it. It has to be spread. Fill me with Your Word, Lord, so that I might share it with others. Please assist me in remembering your Word. Assist me so that I may memorize more and communicate more about you.

In Jesus name, Amen.

DAY #115
EXODUS 37:25-29

25   And he made the incense altar *of* shittim wood: the length of it *was* a cubit, and the breadth of it a cubit; *it was*

foursquare; and two cubits *was* the height of it; the horns thereof were of the same.

26 And he overlaid it with pure gold, *both* the top of it, and the sides thereof round about, and the horns of it: also he made unto it a crown of gold round about.

27 And he made two rings of gold for it under the crown thereof, by the two corners of it, upon the two sides thereof, to be places for the staves to bear it withal.

28 And he made the staves *of* shittim wood, and overlaid them with gold.

29 And he made the holy anointing oil, and the pure incense of sweet spices, according to the work of the apothecary.

The incense altar held the burning incense, which was symbolic of the prayers of the Saints. A sweet savor to God. This central point to where the incense burned could also be representative of Christ. It is because of Him that we have a voice with God. It is because of Him that we can pray and communicate with God.

The oils and incense were something new to Bezaleel. Bezaleel may have acquired help from a perfumer in Israel even though the instructions by God were quite clear. Trying to get things not only right but perfect, it is not wrong to ask for guidance or help.

Dear Lord Jesus,

Help me grasp my prayers to you as a sweet savor. Help me to see them answered. You alone have the ability to answer prayer. You alone have the ability to open my eyes to things unseen. Lord, please put on my heart a burden to pray for the lost. For if you do show me my answered prayers, the greatest of these would be the salvation of others.

In Jesus name, Amen!

DAY #116
EXODUS 38:1-8

1   And he made the altar of burnt offering *of* shittim wood: five cubits *was* the length thereof, and five cubits the breadth thereof; [it was] foursquare; and three cubits the height thereof.
2   And he made the horns thereof on the four corners of it; the horns thereof were of the same: and he overlaid it with brass.
3   And he made all the vessels of the altar, the pots, and the shovels, and the basons, *and* the fleshhooks, and the firepans: all the vessels thereof made he *of* brass.
4   And he made for the altar a brasen grate of network under the compass thereof beneath unto the midst of it.
5   And he cast four rings for the four ends of the grate of brass, *to be* places for the staves.
6   And he made the staves *of* shittim wood, and overlaid them with brass.
7   And he put the staves into the rings on the sides of the altar, to bear it withal; he made the altar hollow with boards.
8   And he made the laver *of* brass, and the foot of it *of* brass, of the looking glasses of [the women] assembling, which assembled *at* the door of the tabernacle of the congregation.

The altar where all sacrifices were offered is described here. After the altar was built, No other altar to God could be built. This one spot upon which all the sins of Israel were addressed. This reminds us that it is only through the blood of Jesus that our sins are forgiven.

Next, the laver is made. It is a work of art made of the mirrors women carried then. Yes, women back then carried mirrors to check how presentable they were. Today you find these mirrors in purses and phones in the self-pic view. The laver was a place where priests were cleansed after the forgiveness of sins. Jesus healed our sinful sickness with His cleansing blood. We receive not only forgiveness of sins but a cleansing that washes away the stain from the sins. Sin leaves a stain. When it is cleansed, that stain is removed. Its punishing problematic power is gone. Only a God who loves beyond description would prepare such a powerful remedy to fix the sinful sickness of man.

Dear Lord Jesus,

May Your love be known throughout the world. Your love is boundless; it can not be caged, restrained, or held. It overwhelms, overpowers, embraces, then overflows. Lord, God almighty, may I never disappoint your love for me. May I be one who points the way to this love of Yours that is so far superior to anything else I know Lord, use me to be one who shares Your incredible love with others.

In Jesus name, Amen.

DAY #117
EXODUS 38:9-20

9   And he made the court: on the south side southward the hangings of the court *were of* fine twined linen, an hundred cubits:

10   Their pillars *were* twenty, and their brasen sockets twenty; the hooks of the pillars and their fillets *were of* silver.

11   And for the north side [the hangings were] an hundred cubits, their pillars *were* twenty, and their sockets of brass twenty; the hooks of the pillars and their fillets *of* silver.

12   And for the west side *were* hangings of fifty cubits, their pillars ten, and their sockets ten; the hooks of the pillars and their fillets *of* silver.

13   And for the east side eastward fifty cubits.

14   The hangings of the one side *of the gate were* fifteen cubits; their pillars three, and their sockets three.

15   And for the other side of the court gate, on this hand and that hand, *were* hangings of fifteen cubits; their pillars three, and their sockets three.

16   All the hangings of the court round about *were* of fine twined linen.

17   And the sockets for the pillars *were of* brass; the hooks of the pillars and their fillets *of* silver; and the overlaying of their chapiters *of* silver; and all the pillars of the court *were* filleted with silver.

18   And the hanging for the gate of the court *was* needlework, *of* blue, and purple, and scarlet, and fine twined linen: and

twenty cubits *was* the length, and the height in the breadth *was* five cubits, answerable to the hangings of the court.

19 And their pillars *were* four, and their sockets *of* brass four; their hooks *of* silver, and the overlaying of their chapiters and their fillets *of* silver.

20 And all the pins of the tabernacle, and of the court round about, *were of* brass.

This part may seem repetitive, but when God repeats something, that means there is something important here. Yes, we read about the curtains of the Tabernacle before. But did we think about the concept of how these pieces connected? Did we think about how easy this is to move from place to place? Did we even dare to think about the concept of broadening it?

Think of the Tabernacle as a church. When it was made, it had room for the Jews only. This meant no one outside of Israel's children could ever serve inside of it.

The church of Christ has accepted any into it who willingly accept that Jesus died for them. Mathew Henry, the great commentator, calls this a fulfillment of Isaiah 54:2-3

> Enlarge the place of your tent, and let them stretch forth the curtains of thine habitations: spare not, lengthen your cords, and strengthen your stakes; For thou shalt break forth on the right hand and on the left; and your seed shall inherit the Gentiles, and make the desolate cities to be inhabited.

Sin is still sin. We do not let up on calling what is evil evil. But the blood of Christ is not restricted to specific people. It is for everyone! This is the GOOD NEWS! This is why we should be singing "Hosanna in the highest!" Now the church is wherever people are that gather in HIS name. Just as the Bible says, "wherever two or three gather in my name, there am I also," so is the church mobile and growing.

Dear Lord Jesus,

I thank You for accepting me as I was, a sinner sick in my desires and lusts. Yet, YOU came and saved me. YOU did this all for me. How can I do any less than share YOUR great love. Lord Jesus, empower me, use me, that I might share this great love of Yours with others.

In Jesus name, Amen.

DAY #118
EXODUS 38:21-31

21 This is the sum of the tabernacle, *even* of the tabernacle of testimony, as it was counted, according to the commandment of Moses, *for* the service of the Levites, by the hand of Ithamar, son to Aaron the priest.

22 And Bezaleel the son of Uri, the son of Hur, of the tribe of Judah, made all that the LORD commanded Moses.

23 And with him *was* Aholiab, son of Ahisamach, of the tribe of Dan, an engraver, and a cunning workman, and an embroiderer in blue, and in purple, and in scarlet, and fine linen.

24 All the gold that was occupied for the work in all the work of the holy *place*, even the gold of the offering, was twenty and nine talents, and seven hundred and thirty shekels, after the shekel of the sanctuary.
25 And the silver of them that were numbered of the congregation *was* an hundred talents, and a thousand seven hundred and threescore and fifteen shekels, after the shekel of the sanctuary:
26 A bekah for every man, *that is*, half a shekel, after the shekel of the sanctuary, for every one that went to be numbered, from twenty years old and upward, for six hundred thousand and three thousand and five hundred and fifty *men*.
27 And of the hundred talents of silver were cast the sockets of the sanctuary, and the sockets of the vail; an hundred sockets of the hundred talents, a talent for a socket.
28 And of the thousand seven hundred seventy and five shekels he made hooks for the pillars, and overlaid their chapiters, and filleted them.
29 And the brass of the offering *was* seventy talents, and two thousand and four hundred shekels.
30 And therewith he made the sockets to the door of the tabernacle of the congregation, and the brasen altar, and the brasen grate for it, and all the vessels of the altar,
31 And the sockets of the court round about, and the sockets of the court gate, and all the pins of the tabernacle, and all the pins of the court round about.

Here we see one of the first examples of financial accountability ever recorded. Ithamar, Aaron's son, was responsible for counting and keeping track of all that was donated. This accounting must have been thought of at the time as important. But could Ithamar have ever grasped this one report he wrote would one day be part of scripture?

How well do we do the tasks that are assigned to us? Do we think of each and everything that falls to us as important, so important that God might be checking in on it? DO we dare to think about how God will look as people look at us and our work? Sometimes we simply are tired and must press on, but this does not mean the quality of what we can do less than our best.

When we stop caring about our work, we stop caring about being given an important task by God. Every little deed, even if it is cleaning a toilet, sweeping the floor, washing the dishes, fixing a car, etc., is important! We need to do everything we do for the glory of God. We need to fight that battle within ourselves that says our work is meaningless and no one will ever see it so that we begin to think that all of our work will be on display with the world, and people will begin to see Jesus because of the quality of our work.

Dear Lord Jesus,

Please help me to see how important the mundane and tiresome, boring tasks I have been assigned are to You. Help me to see that each and every little thing I am asked to do reflects on how great YOU are, not me. Lord, please work on me so that I will begin to do my best in everything I do. Please change my attitude so that I begin to see everything I do as glorifying You!

In Jesus name, Amen.

DAY #119
EXODUS 39:1-31

1 And of the blue, and purple, and scarlet, they made cloths of service, to do service in the holy *place*, and made the holy garments for Aaron; as the LORD commanded Moses.
2 And he made the ephod *of* gold, blue, and purple, and scarlet, and fine twined linen.
3 And they did beat the gold into thin plates, and cut *it into* wires, to work *it* in the blue, and in the purple, and in the scarlet, and in the fine linen, *with* cunning work.
4 They made shoulder pieces for it, to couple *it* together: by the two edges was it coupled together.
5 And the curious girdle of his ephod, that *was* upon it, *was* of the same, according to the work thereof; *of* gold, blue, and purple, and scarlet, and fine twined linen; as the LORD commanded Moses.
6 And they wrought onyx stones inclosed in ouches of gold, graven, as signets are graven, with the names of the children of Israel.
7 And he put them on the shoulders of the ephod, *that they should be* stones for a memorial to the children of Israel; as the LORD commanded Moses.
8 And he made the breastplate *of* cunning work, like the work of the ephod; *of* gold, blue, and purple, and scarlet, and fine twined linen.
9 It was foursquare; they made the breastplate double: a span *was* the length thereof, and a span the breadth thereof, *being* doubled.
10 And they set in it four rows of stones: *the first* row *was* a sardius, a topaz, and a carbuncle: this *was* the first row.
11 And the second row, an emerald, a sapphire, and a diamond.
12 And the third row, a ligure, an agate, and an amethyst.

13   And the fourth row, a beryl, an onyx, and a jasper: *they were* inclosed in ouches of gold in their inclosings.
14   And the stones *were* according to the names of the children of Israel, twelve, according to their names, *like* the engravings of a signet, every one with his name, according to the twelve tribes.
15   And they made upon the breastplate chains at the ends, *of* wreathen work *of* pure gold.
16   And they made two ouches *of* gold, and two gold rings; and put the two rings in the two ends of the breastplate.
17   And they put the two wreathen chains of gold in the two rings on the ends of the breastplate.
18   And the two ends of the two wreathen chains they fastened in the two ouches, and put them on the shoulder pieces of the ephod, before it.
19   And they made two rings of gold, and put *them* on the two ends of the breastplate, upon the border of it, which *was* on the side of the ephod inward.
20   And they made two *other* golden rings, and put them on the two sides of the ephod underneath, toward the forepart of it, over against the *other* coupling thereof, above the curious girdle of the ephod.
21   And they did bind the breastplate by his rings unto the rings of the ephod with a lace of blue, that it might be above the curious girdle of the ephod, and that the breastplate might not be loosed from the ephod; as the LORD commanded Moses.
22   And he made the robe of the ephod *of* woven work, all *of* blue.
23   And *there was* an hole in the midst of the robe, as the hole of an habergeon, *with* a band round about the hole, that it should not rend.

24   And they made upon the hems of the robe pomegranates *of* blue, and purple, and scarlet, *and* twined [linen].
25   And they made bells *of* pure gold, and put the bells between the pomegranates upon the hem of the robe, round about between the pomegranates;
26   A bell and a pomegranate, a bell and a pomegranate, round about the hem of the robe to minister *in*; as the LORD commanded Moses.
27   And they made coats *of* fine linen *of* woven work for Aaron, and for his sons,
28   And a mitre *of* fine linen, and goodly bonnets *of* fine linen, and linen breeches *of* fine twined linen,
29   And a girdle *of* fine twined linen, and blue, and purple, and scarlet, *of* needlework; as the LORD commanded Moses.
30   And they made the plate of the holy crown *of* pure gold, and wrote upon it a writing, [like to] the engravings of a signet, HOLINESS TO THE LORD.
31   And they tied unto it a lace of blue, to fasten *it* on high upon the mitre; as the LORD commanded Moses.

The last of the things prepared, or the last of the things accounted for are the garments of the high priest and those that serve in the Tabernacle. There are some things I was curious about when I read the description of these clothes given to Moses. Here my curiosity was satisfied. My brain was contemplating how they were able to get the gold into the designs for the cloth. I pondered how they would get a thread to take on gold without burning the thread. Yet, here in vs. 3. they explain how they did this.

The details of how are here. The details of the garment's completion are here. But the one thing that may be the most important is in verse 1:

... they made cloths of service, to do service in the holy place, and made the holy garments for Aaron; as the LORD commanded Moses.

Wearing these garments was a high honor; the highest honor in all of Israel. Yet, these garments, these clothes are not described as honorable. They are not described as works of art, they are described as "cloths of service." Service to do God's bidding and service to the people. The high priest could bring the people's needs and concerns to the Lord.

Clothing is what others see us wearing. How do people see us? Do they see us as serving God? Do they see us as having a kind heart?

Dear Lord Jesus,

Please, Lord, guide us to having a humbleness. Take from us pompousness, stuffiness, false pride, and all manner of showiness. Lord, help us to be small that YOU may shine. Lord, let all that is important about us be about YOU. Let us not be braggarts. But let us be the ones who brag on Your splendor.

In Jesus name, Amen.

DAY #120
EXODUS 39:32-43

32 Thus was all the work of the tabernacle of the tent of the congregation finished: and the children of Israel did according to all that the LORD commanded Moses, so did they.
33 And they brought the tabernacle unto Moses, the tent, and all his furniture, his taches, his boards, his bars, and his pillars, and his sockets,
34 And the covering of rams' skins dyed red, and the covering of badgers' skins, and the vail of the covering,
35 The ark of the testimony, and the staves thereof, and the mercy seat,
36 The table, *and* all the vessels thereof, and the shewbread,
37 The pure candlestick, *with* the lamps thereof, [even with] the lamps to be set in order, and all the vessels thereof, and the oil for light,
38 And the golden altar, and the anointing oil, and the sweet incense, and the hanging for the tabernacle door,
39 The brasen altar, and his grate of brass, his staves, and all his vessels, the laver and his foot,
40 The hangings of the court, his pillars, and his sockets, and the hanging for the court gate, his cords, and his pins, and all the vessels of the service of the tabernacle, for the tent of the congregation,
41 The cloths of service to do service in the holy *place*, and the holy garments for Aaron the priest, and his sons' garments, to minister in the priest's office.
42 According to all that the LORD commanded Moses, so the children of Israel made all the work.
43 And Moses did look upon all the work, and, behold, they had done it as the LORD had commanded, even so had they done it: and Moses blessed them.

Can you imagine the day the work was completed and ready to be delivered to Moses? The day has arrived when all of these outstanding artisans' work could finally be revealed. Do you think they told everyone that day had arrived? Only two names are recorded—those who managed the projects. Yet, the number of workers was extensive. Matthew Henry states this work was completed within 5 months. The highly detailed artistic touch of those who had been loved and forgiven by God was emblazoned on the completed works. A planned parade, no. These workers were humble; they were proud that they were included in the project. But since the people around had to notice what was happening, there was likely a huge audience.

No mention is made of having met a deadline or beating it. No comment is made here other than, *"behold, they had done it as the LORD had commanded, even so, had they done it: and Moses blessed them."* Is there any greater compliment to receive than to be told, "you have done as the LORD commanded" How many of us can say that when we finish a project? We need to ask ourselves, "Did I do this work as if I was delivering this project to God?" Sometimes deadlines force us to not do our best work. In those cases, ask yourself if you did the best you could in the time you were given.

But can you say the quality of your work is the best you can do? If so, are you striving to learn more and do better at what you do? Perhaps the question we need to ask ourselves is, "how do we make our work stand out as the best?"

Dear Lord Jesus,

Help me to excel in my work and in the way I show my love to my family. Lord, help me to be Your example in how I live my life and how I do my work. Sometimes that means setting aside work to be with my children. Help me to know these things. Help me set things right. Lord, use me that how I live and love makes YOU stand out all the more to those around me.

In Jesus name, Amen.

www.ingramcontent.com/pod-product-compliance
Lightning Source LLC
LaVergne TN
LVHW010215070526
838199LV00062B/4599